UNTAPPED

UNTAPPED

Creating Value in Underserved Markets

John Weiser
Steve Rochlin
Michele Kahane
Jessica Landis

BERRETT-KOEHLER PUBLISHERS, INC.
San Francisco

Berrett-Koehler Publishers, Inc.
235 Montgomery Street, Suite 650
San Francisco, CA 94104-2916
Tel: (415) 288-0260   Fax: (415) 362-2512   www.bkconnection.com

Ordering Information
Quantity sales. Special discounts are available on quantity purchases by corporations, associations, and others. For details, contact the "Special Sales Department" at the Berrett-Koehler address above.
Individual sales. Berrett-Koehler publications are available through most bookstores. They can also be ordered directly from Berrett-Koehler: Tel: (800) 929-2929; Fax: (802) 864-7626; www.bkconnection.com
Orders for college textbook/course adoption use. Please contact Berrett-Koehler: Tel: (800) 929-2929; Fax: (802) 864-7626.
Orders by U.S. trade bookstores and wholesalers. Please contact Publishers Group West, 1700 Fourth Street, Berkeley, CA 94710. Tel: (510) 528-1444; Fax: (510) 528-3444.

Berrett-Koehler and the BK logo are registered trademarks of Berrett-Koehler Publishers, Inc.

Printed in the United States of America

Berrett-Koehler books are printed on long-lasting acid-free paper. When it is available, we choose paper that has been manufactured by environmentally responsible processes. These may include using trees grown in sustainable forests, incorporating recycled paper, minimizing chlorine in bleaching, or recycling the energy produced at the paper mill.

Library of Congress Cataloging-in-Publication Data
Untapped : creating value in underserved markets / by John Weiser . . . [et al.].
    p. cm.
  Includes bibliographical references and index.
  Contents: Contents: Tapping new markets—Recruiting and retaining a qualified workforce—Increasing value in the supply chain—Accelerating product and process innovation—Building partnerships that work—Creating value for business and community.
    ISBN-10: 1–57675–372–7; ISBN-13: 978–1–57675–372–9
    1. Success in business.   2. Social responsibility of business.   3. Business logistics.   I. Weiser, John, 1955–
HF5386.U517 2006
658.4'01—dc22   2005057121

First Edition
11 10 09 08 07 06   10 9 8 7 6 5 4 3 2 1
Copyedited by Alice Vigliani, Alice Vigliani and Associates. Composition and production services by Westchester Book Group. Index by Seth Maislin, Focus Information Services.

We dedicate this book to our spouses and loved ones:

Shoshana Zax

Christina Sevilla

Benjamin Lapp

Jean and Phil Landis

Your help, attention, and support have sustained us through the long process of distilling years of experience into written text. Thank you for your patience, your fortitude, and most of all, your love.

❏ CONTENTS

❑ PREFACE AND ACKNOWLEDGEMENTS

Tapping underserved markets for consumers, for employees, or for suppliers is not a new idea in business. On the contrary, it's central to business success and growth. When Henry Ford founded the Ford Motor Company in 1903, he proclaimed, "I will build a car for the great multitude." Ford helped evolve the car from luxury item for the well-to-do to essential transportation for the ordinary man or woman by changing manufacturing processes to lower production costs and, therefore, the price of cars. Similarly, adapting workplace and supply chain management practices to integrate more diverse labor pools and suppliers—for example, women and minorities—is now seen as essential to business success.

The attention of the business world has focused more sharply in recent years on creating business opportunities in underserved markets. The *Harvard Business Review, Sloan Management Review, The Economist,* and *Forbes* have all featured articles on efforts to reach underserved communities. A group of leading thinkers have helped develop and clarify the business case for investing in underserved markets, including C. K. Prahalad (University of Michigan), Stuart Hart (Cornell), Al Hammond (World Resources Institute), and Clayton Christensen (Harvard). They have demonstrated the tremendous market opportunity in selling to underserved communities at the "bottom of the pyramid" (BOP)—the 4 to 5 billion people worldwide living on $2 a day. In their work, they argue that to be profitable, firms cannot simply fine-tune the products they already sell to rich customers. Instead, they must re-engineer products to reflect the very different economics of the BOP: small unit packages, low margin, high volume.

In the United States, Michael Porter (Harvard) and his affiliate organization, the Initiative for a Competitive Inner City, among others, have made strong arguments for the competitive advantages of business investment in the inner cities of the United States. Other authors such as Simon Zadek, Jane Nelson, and David Grayson, and research from the World Business Council for Sustainable Development, Business for Social Responsibility, the International Business Leaders Forum, the United Nations Global Compact, and the World Economic Forum have focused on the business risks and opportunities created by crucial issues emerging in the areas of the environment, health, diversity, and human rights and the critical role of partnerships between business, nonprofits, and government in addressing these issues.

Untapped is built on this intellectual foundation. Some of the book's unique features are listed below:

- *Oriented to managers.* We have tried to provide practical guidance to the business manager. To date, much of the literature has focused on making the business case for these activities but has been short on providing a solid business model—the practical do's and don'ts that every manager needs before starting down a new path. This book fills that void by providing concise and clear lessons from businesses that have successfully invested in underserved markets. We have developed a five-point strategic management framework based on hundreds of case studies. Within this framework, we illustrate both successes and failures across a wide range of industries and geographies.

- *Inclusive of all business functions.* Unlike most other articles and books that focus on sales alone (and on the low-income individual as a consumer), our work addresses all the business functions that can benefit from investment in underserved communities. This includes not only sales but also human resources, brand and reputation management, product development, and purchasing. We give specific strategies for success for each of these business functions, distilled from the experience of companies in our case studies.

- *Focused on the whole market system.* Firms operate in complex market systems. We try to illustrate how business executives can manage different internal factors (e.g., performance incentives, cross-functional teams) and the external factors (e.g., competition, public policy, and strategic partners) to succeed in underserved markets.

- *Includes U.S. and European underserved communities.* The examples we use are drawn from the U.S. and European context (about two-thirds of the cases) and from the developing world (about one-third). This adds to the current literature, which has largely focused on underserved markets in developing countries. Recent events in both the United States (Hurricane Katrina) and Europe (riots in France among ethnic minorities) provide a vivid reminder that low-income and underserved communities exist right in the backyards of global corporations. We believe the book shines a light on these forgotten communities. We also believe that much learning can be done across geographic boundaries, albeit recognizing that one must always be sensitive to local context.

Many of the cases in this book, and many of the lessons learned, were drawn from the Ford Foundation's Corporate Involvement (CI) Initiative. The Ford Foundation launched the CI Initiative in 1995 to demonstrate how business and communities could collaborate to generate win-win outcomes—competitive advantage for business, and gains in assets and wealth for low-income people. Since then, the Ford Foundation has invested in a group of innovative organizations (companies, NGOs, think tanks, and business associations) that have spearheaded the practice of doing business in underserved markets. A number of this book's authors were involved closely in the implementation of this multi-year initiative. Together with the close to 50 organizations supported by the CI Initiative, we built an active community of practice from which many of the insights in this book were derived.

Our book is meant to confer practical information about how to reach underserved markets in both developed and developing countries. Our aim is to reach senior decision makers and managers in corporations and help them do their job better. But this is only part of our objective. We also care deeply about making the world a better place for all. And we are passionate in the belief that business can be an agent for value creation that benefits not only shareholders but also society more broadly. This book is not about corporate philanthropy. It is about how business can make a profit *and* make a dramatic economic difference in the lives of the poor through its everyday business decisions—what products it makes, to whom it sells its products, who it chooses to employ, where it locates, from whom it procures goods and services. While corporate philanthropy is important, business can make an even greater contribution to society through its core competencies and activities. Consider the following: in the United States, total corporate philanthropy was $12 billion in 2004, while total purchasing from minority-owned businesses in the same year was $87 billion. This shows the scale of the impact that can be developed when the core operating activities of businesses are brought to bear.

The book is based on over a combined 60 years of the authors' experience. We are a diverse group, drawing from our work in and with businesses, nonprofits, government, and philanthropy. We believe the fact that each of us has straddled all these sectors at some time in our careers has provided us with a unique vantage point from which to explore the issues addressed in this work.

We would like to acknowledge and thank the many individuals who have contributed their thoughts and ideas to this book. In particular, we would like to thank the Ford Foundation, and especially Frank DeGiovanni. A generous grant from the Ford Foundation made writing this book possible. In addition, the undertaking would have been impossible without the active engagement and assistance of all of the participants in the Ford Foundation Corporate Involvement Initiative, and we thank them all for their time, energy, and leadership.

We would like to thank the Center for Corporate Citizenship at Boston College for its willingness to support its staff in writing this book, and the support of its communications team in creating opportunities to inform the center's corporate members of our ideas.

We also would like to thank staff at Laufer, Green, Isaac for their assistance in informing businesses about these ideas.

We particularly would like to thank the individuals who encouraged us to write this book and who took the time to read drafts of our work: Jim Austin, Bill Boler, Peter Brew, Sasha Dichter, Bob Dunn, Jeff Hamaoui, Scott Hudson, Donna Klein, Ken Lehman, Jonathan Levine, Kimmo Lipponen, Kellie McElhaney, Todd Manza, Don Mayer, Lee Morgan, Celina Pagani-Tousignant, Rick Peyser, Diane Stoneman, Lynda Talgo, Alis Valencia, Bob Weissbourd, Celeste Wroblewski, and Simon Zadek. We also would like to thank Andy Lewandowski and Ellen West for their invaluable assistance.

Ultimately, this book is indebted to the creative risk-taking of the people behind the stories discussed in these pages. We thank them for the opportunity to learn from their experience, and we thank Berrett-Koehler (and especially Johanna Vondeling) for the opportunity to tell their story.

John Weiser
Steve Rochlin
Michele Kahane
Jessica Landis
Branford, Connecticut
May 2006

INTRODUCTION: FINDING THE OPPORTUNITIES

Domestic and international underserved markets represent a multi-trillion-dollar opportunity that is largely untapped. This market has some of the fastest-growing companies and fastest-growing business opportunities. It is also a market with the fastest-growing workforce and a rapidly expanding supplier base.

If you are interested in increasing your company's activities in these markets and want to know how to create business value and avoid business risks, this book is for you. We have distilled the experience of hundreds of companies operating in underserved markets in both developed and developing countries. By *underserved markets*, we mean communities in which there is a high percentage of low-income individuals, or a high percentage of ethnic minorities, or both. From the wealth of case studies we have reviewed, we have developed a set of five success factors that you can use to guide your company to profitable operations. We show you how to apply these success factors to each of four business disciplines: sales and marketing, human resources, purchasing, and product and process innovation. As the diagram below shows, individuals in underserved markets can have multiple potential relationships with business, including customer, employee, supplier, and neighbor. These business disciplines help show the span of ways that companies and communities can create mutually beneficial relationships. We pre-

A Corporation's Relationship with the Community

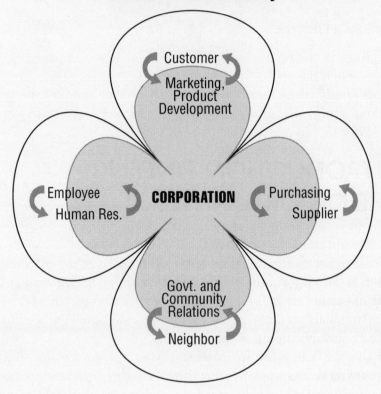

sent many business examples that can help you understand how the success factors work in companies in a variety of industries and locations.

Are you somewhat skeptical that this approach might work well for your company? Consider the following four case studies of companies that created business value in these markets. The case studies cover both large and small companies, headquartered both inside as well as outside the United States. Consider also the following cautionary tale—an example of a foray into these markets that didn't succeed initially. The cases we describe not only will give you a more detailed understanding of the kind of success that is possible, but also will signal what kinds of pitfalls to avoid. In addition, they illustrate the five success factors.

SALES: CITIBANK

Citigroup is one of the largest financial services companies in the world. When Banamex, Mexico's leading bank, merged into the Citigroup family of financial companies in 2001, Citibank, the retail banking arm of Citigroup, began to explore ways to create a profitable product in the market for remittances—transfers from immigrants to relatives abroad. In April 2003, Citibank introduced Citibank Global Transfers, which offers U.S. bank customers convenient money transfers domestically or to Mexico for a flat $5 fee—a significant discount from the fees of the major competitors. Citibank was able to offer this product profitably because it already had the infrastructure in place to move money inexpensively from customer accounts to ATMs anyplace in the world.

But there was a catch—this only worked if the sender was a Citibank customer and if the recipient had an ATM card. Many of the individuals sending remittances from the United States had no banking relationship at all, and many of the recipients did not have ATM cards. To reach this market segment, Citibank adapted its business model to develop a two-part solution. The most significant adaptation was the creation of the Citibank Access Account, a "checkless checking account" with features that made it attractive for immigrants to open an account with Citibank. The second adaptation was the Banamex Tricolor Card, which enabled recipients of the transferred funds in Mexico to access the funds through Banamex branches, ATMs, or debit card channels throughout the country, safely and efficiently.

By adapting its business model, Citibank has been able to successfully create a relationship that has value for both the bank and the community. The bank has tens of thousands of new, profitable customers. And immigrants in the United States, as well as their relatives in Mexico, have a lower-cost alternative for sending home funds safely and securely. As a testament to the attractiveness of this approach, consider the fact that in 2004, Citizens Bank and Sovereign Bank launched similar products (First Data, 2004).

HUMAN RESOURCES: MANPOWER

Manpower is a worldwide leader in the staffing industry, with client firms that include 94 percent of the Fortune 500. In 1999, Manpower determined that it needed to develop a strategic national workforce development program to address long-term information technology (IT) employment needs in the United States by tapping the workforce in underserved communities. Despite the current downturn in demand for IT workers, the U.S. Bureau of Labor Statistics projects that IT employment will nearly double from 2.1 million jobs in 2000 to 3.9 million jobs by 2010 in the United States. Clearly, Manpower's business model succeeds or fails based on its ability to deliver qualified workers to client employer companies. A labor pool shortage like the one of the 1990s could hurt the company's profitability.

In response to this problem, Manpower initiated TechReach, a strategic workforce development program. The program is employer driven; participants are trained in specific skill sets required by employers in each program's local area, increasing the likelihood of program graduates' placement upon their completion of the program.

In May 2003, Manpower formed a National Business Partnership with the U.S. Department of Labor, which linked thousands of local Manpower offices with the local Department of Labor branches. By creating this partnership, Manpower was able to expand the level of activity and impact of the TechReach program. Manpower is now placing thousands of individuals per year into jobs through its TechReach program. Since Manpower earns its fees through placement of individuals into jobs, this has created new profit opportunities for Manpower in addition to new job opportunities for individuals from underserved communities (Center for Corporate Citizenship, 2003; Ford Foundation, 2005).

PURCHASING: GREEN MOUNTAIN COFFEE ROASTERS

Green Mountain Coffee Roasters (GMCR) is a Vermont-based wholesale coffee company that roasts more than 75 high-quality arabica coffees. It had sales of $137 million in FY 2004 and has been recognized by *Forbes* magazine in the years 2002 to 2004 as one of the "200 Best Small Companies in America."

In an effort to reach new customers, Green Mountain added "Fair Trade"certified coffees to its product line. Coffee that meets the Fair Trade standard is purchased under prices and terms that enable farmers in underserved markets to earn a sustainable livelihood and produce a high-quality bean. Coffee that is sold in the U.S. markets is certified to meet the standards by TransFair USA, an independent certification organization.

Green Mountain has been able to use the Fair Trade certified standard to differentiate its coffee from other coffees that are not Fair Trade certified. And even though Fair Trade coffee is more expensive to purchase, the company has been able to set a price that enables it to make a good profit.

The Fair Trade and Organic certified line is now Green Mountain's fastest-growing product line, accounting for approximately 16 percent of its sales in FY 2004. And recently, Green Mountain Coffee announced its goal of having 35 percent of its coffee sales be Fair Trade and Organic certified by the end of FY 2008.

Fair Trade coffee has created business value for Green Mountain Coffee Roasters because it has enabled the company to expand profitably. And it has created value for small-farm coffee growers in underserved markets because it has helped ensure that their product is purchased on terms that let them earn a sustainable livelihood (Ford Foundation, 2005).

PRODUCT DEVELOPMENT: CEMEX

The development of CEMEX's Patrimonio Hoy product line is a good example of product development that has led to dramatically increased sales. In the mid-1990s, CEMEX, which is the world's second-largest cement maker and one of Mexico's largest companies, was hit hard by Mexico's crippling currency devaluation. The buying power of the peso was cut almost in half, dramatically reducing the market for CEMEX's products.

The company decided to pursue increased sales in the do-it-yourself homebuilding market, which dominates the lower-income neighborhoods in Mexico. In order to create a new product offering, the company significantly changed its typical process for gathering information on customer needs, sending a team of managers to live in these neighborhoods for a year. This innovative approach led to the creation of the "Patrimonio Hoy" group purchasing program, which combined financing, architectural advice, and building materials into one package. CEMEX worked with the customers to form buying clubs. Each member of the club would pay a small portion of his or her earnings into the club each week, and then, on a regular basis, the pooled money would be used to make a purchase from Patrimonio Hoy. This approach enabled consumers to pay for building supplies from their weekly earnings and to get advice on how to use them most effectively.

The results from the experience of the first 1,000 families in the purchasing program were dramatic. Whereas an average homebuilder had traditionally built one room every four to seven years, members of CEMEX's group purchasing program took an average of one and a half years, less than a third of the time. Not only was the speed of building (and therefore the sale of building materials) accelerated, but also as a result of the program 18 percent more families in the test region had begun building, and the average annual spending per family increased from $240 to almost $600. Families planned to build two to three more rooms than they had originally, and their constructions now contained 25 percent more cement per cubic meter. The families also used materials more efficiently because they were able to get the right amount of materials for the rooms that they planned, and they lost less material in wastage. The CEMEX program created value for communities because it helped families build housing more quickly, more efficiently, and more safely. And it has created business value for CEMEX by tapping into a market that the company couldn't reach effectively before.

Based on this initial success, CEMEX expanded the program quickly, and it now has 70,000 Mexican families enrolled in the program. CEMEX is planning to expand the program to other countries as well (CEMEX, 2005; Sandoval, 2005; Vision, 2005).

A CAUTIONARY TALE

The pathway to developing profitable opportunities in underserved markets is not always straight and easy to follow. There are numerous examples of companies that attempted to create businesses in underserved markets, only to have them collapse or be delayed for years. Pathmark's move into Harlem is a classic example. In the early 1990s, Pathmark saw a significant opportunity to open a major supermarket in Harlem. Its profitable experiences in other underserved neighborhoods helped it to see promise where others saw only problems. It worked together with several local community groups to develop a plan for putting a supermarket on a parcel of empty city-owned land on 125th Street, a major thoroughfare with good access to subway and bus transportation. Market studies showed that more than 60 percent of Harlem's retail spending occurred outside the neighborhood, suggesting a high level of untapped demand. And Pathmark had honed its product line for African American neighborhoods with stores in similar locations, such as Bedford-Stuyvesant.

But political resistance to the Pathmark store was organized by the owners of "bodegas"—small local convenience stores catering to the neighborhood residents—and by the major wholesaler who supplied those stores. Together, they were able to mount a campaign of political resistance that slowed the store development to a crawl for many years. They portrayed Pathmark as a greedy, uncaring corporation that was going to drive local business owners bankrupt. They also played on racial and ethnic tensions.

The deal was eventually approved by the city council, but only after Pathmark's community partners, particularly the Abyssinian Black Baptist Church, were able to show residents that the benefits to the community as a whole were considerable and the losses to merchants were likely to be small. Pathmark would reduce grocery costs significantly for residents and would create hundreds of well-paying jobs. And even though it would complete with local merchants, the majority of Harlem residents' grocery dollars were currently spent outside the neighborhood. Pathmark would really be competing with the bigger stores outside Harlem, not with the bodegas. After an extraordinarily tense 7–5 city council vote, the deal was approved. Construction was able to take place, and the store opened in 1999. The store is now profitable, and Pathmark has moved forward on several additional stores in New York City ethnic neighborhoods. In addition, development has taken off on 125th Street. The street now offers residents a major shopping mall including stores such as HMV, Modell, Old Navy, CVS, Disney, Costco, and Staples (Grunewald, 1999; Thomas, 2003; WinWinPartner.com, 2005).

SUCCESS FACTORS

As the previous examples indicate, there is both opportunity and risk in underserved markets. How do you seize the opportunities without succumbing to the risks? Our research provides the answers. This book is drawn from seven years of research and market testing with trailblazing companies on how to successfully adapt to the specific conditions in underserved markets. This research—organized and supported by the Ford Foundation—sought to find ways to increase corporate engagement with underserved communities in ways that created economic benefits for both communities and business. The companies in our research sample were primarily large, and approximately three-quarters were headquartered in the United States. Clearly, our lessons are most applicable to similar companies. But the research also indicates that our lessons can be adapted, both to large corporations based outside the United States as well as to smaller businesses located in the United States (Ford Foundation, 2005).

If we had to put everything we have learned into a nutshell, we would say that the most important overarching success factor is to create value for the community at the same time as you create value for business. You must create a "win-win" relationship with the communities in which you do business. For companies, the win can take the form of increased sales, reduced costs, diversification of risk, or improvements in reputation. For communities, the win can take the form of access to needed goods and services, jobs, or entrepreneurial opportunities. If you only remember one thing from this book, remember this: *a win-win relationship is everything.*

This is evident in the case studies above. In each of the four successful cases, the company was able to find a way to create value for itself *and* value for the consumers, suppliers, and residents of the community. In the cautionary tale, Pathmark's development was stalled because vocal elements of the community were able to paint its entry into the market as a "win-lose" relationship. Pathmark was only able to move forward when it created a win-win relationship with a key partner in the community.

In fact, more than two-thirds of the companies in our research that successfully tapped underserved markets had formed a partnership with an organization that brought new knowledge, skills, resources, or connections to their effort. These partnerships were with a wide range of organizations, including other businesses, government agencies, nonprofit organizations, and community groups. Frequently, these organizations were drawn to working with the companies because they were seeking to create community benefits rather than trying to make a profit themselves.

But you may still be feeling a little skeptical. Yes, of course, having a win-win relationship makes it a lot easier to establish an enduring profitable business in a community. That's true of every community, not just underserved ones. But how do you create a profitable and mutually beneficial relationship with these communities?

That's where the five success factors come in. We examined hundreds of case studies from companies in these markets, some of which did extraordinarily well and some much less so. We were able to distill five factors that distinguished superior performance from mediocre performance in underserved markets:

1. Mine and translate local market information.
2. Adapt business model to community realities.
3. Change internal incentives and challenge cultural assumptions.
4. Create partnerships and strategic alliances.
5. Improve the enabling environment.

■ I. MINE AND TRANSLATE LOCAL MARKET INFORMATION

You already know that information, both about the market and about your company's performance, is critical to ensure your ability to identify opportunities, avoid pitfalls, and take corrective action where necessary. What you may not know is that your company most likely will need to change some of the ways it "mines" information in underserved markets. It may need to collect different types of information, or collect information from nontraditional sources. It also is likely that your company will need to analyze the information in a somewhat different way for these markets than for mainstream markets. The same information, in two different markets, may carry different meanings. For example, government-reported statistics on household income can convey a quite different meaning in a low-income urban neighborhood than in a well-to-do suburban neighborhood. Analyzing it the same way can lead to flawed decisions. Your company must learn how to "translate" the information to carry out accurate analysis in these markets.

This is clearly evident in the CEMEX example. Instead of using its standard approaches to gathering and analyzing data for product development, the company sent managers to live in the communities to understand how individuals already planned and financed their "do-it-yourself" projects. This firsthand knowledge led to the development of an entirely new approach to selling cement to low-income households.

■ 2. ADAPT BUSINESS MODEL TO COMMUNITY REALITIES

The business model that is used to sell fine dining is different from the one used to sell fast food. In the same way, the business model your company uses currently for its sales and marketing, for hiring, and the like will need to be adapted and extended for underserved markets. Your company will likely need to adapt product features and benefits, distribution channels, marketing approaches, and price points. The Citibank example demonstrates this point—it needed to change the way that it bundled product features, and it had to adapt its distribution channels in order to develop a product offering that could reach new markets.

■ 3. CHANGE INTERNAL INCENTIVES AND CHALLENGE   CULTURAL ASSUMPTIONS

Your company probably has developed a set of financial and social incentives that help to align the behaviors of all of its employees with its strategic goals and objectives. These incentives may need to be adjusted in order to help generate the right behaviors in underserved markets. Incentives might have to shift, for example, from a focus on margins to a focus on total profits in order to encourage managers to spend time and energy building business in these markets that might be lower margin.

Employees of your company also have a tacit set of cultural assumptions, which are generated through their own personal experience and history. These assumptions may need to be challenged if they include inaccuracies or biases concerning underserved individuals and communities. For example, the introduction of Fair Trade coffee by Green Mountain Coffee Roasters occurred after a year of challenging internal debates over whether customers would truly value coffee purchased on a Fair Trade basis. The initial sales also required education of employees, distributors, and end-user customers. They needed to understand how Fair Trade coffee was different, and why that difference was worth paying more for. This understanding was developed through case examples, customer testimonies, focus groups, mailings, articles, and websites.

■ 4. CREATE PARTNERSHIPS AND STRATEGIC ALLIANCES

In many of the markets in which it operates, your company probably has developed strategic alliances and partnerships with suppliers, customers, brokers, and other key market participants in order to leverage value and increase sales and profits. Underserved markets are no different. Our research shows that the development of partnerships and alliances with businesses, nonprofits, and governmental agencies is often critical to success in these markets. Such organizations can help your company reach customers, find workers, develop sources of supply, and create profitable new products and processes. For example, the strategic partnership between Manpower and the U.S. Department of Labor helped Manpower to identify potential individuals for job placement much more efficiently and quickly than it could using its traditional sources of supply.

■ 5. IMPROVE THE ENABLING ENVIRONMENT

The enabling environment—the laws, institutions, and infrastructure that support (or hinder) business activity in a market—often need to be improved in order to do business profitably in underserved markets. Businesses can and do often play an effective role in helping to improve this environment. Often, the most effective approach is to work in collaboration with other businesses and nonprofit advocacy groups to identify key problems and develop the political will to make effective change. This is true whether the underserved market is an inner city in the United States or a rural community in a developing country. The web of laws and infrastructure often needs to be shaped in ways that permit a mutually beneficial relationship to be realized. While this was not a major theme in the case studies noted above, we will give many examples, such as the WINs case study near the end of Chapter 2, in the rest of the book.

The following chapters examine each of these five success factors in detail, showing you how to apply them in each of four business functions: sales and marketing, human resources, purchasing, and product and process innovation. These four business functions cover the range of relationships that people in underserved markets have with businesses: as consumers, employees, suppliers, and neighbors.

For each success factor and each business function, we consider what's different about underserved markets and how to apply the success factor to address the challenges created by these differences. We illustrate with many short case examples. At the end of each chapter on a business function, we provide a longer case study showing how one company used multiple success factors to create a profitable operation in an underserved market while creating benefits for the company as well. We also identify specific measures that can be used to track your success in the markets.

Because win-win partnerships are so important, we devote a whole chapter to the do's and don'ts of building and managing partnerships. Chapter 5 gives you an in-depth look at how to start a partnership, manage an ongoing partnership, and wind up a partnership that has achieved its objectives.

We end the book with a chapter that provides a summary and a synthesis showing how to use the five success factors in a versatile way across the different business units.

By the time you finish reading this book, you will know how to invest and partner with underserved communities to both create significant competitive advantages for your company and build vibrant communities in which to live, work, and do business. You will know how to create value for business and value for these communities as well.

TAPPING NEW MARKETS

Are you interested in increasing the profitable sales of your products and services? Are you thinking about opportunities in underserved markets—but cautious about potential risks and barriers? If your answer is yes, then this chapter is for you.

Many managers of marketing and sales have concerns about being able to increase profitable sales in underserved markets. They ask questions such as: Are there actually enough customers with enough buying power to make the marketing effort worthwhile? Can my company deliver products and services with the right mix of features and benefits at the right price points to win sales in this market? Will my company's brand—which is strong enough to support a premium over the "generic" brand in the mainstream market—have value in this community?

This chapter provides insights and approaches that will enable you to answer questions like these for your own company. We take the five success factors identified in the Introduction and show you how to translate them for use in the sales and marketing context in underserved populations. We also illustrate these success factors with examples from companies such as Hewlett-Packard, Hindustan Lever, Shaw's, Safeco, JPMorgan Chase, and Fannie Mae, which have all succeeded in developing profitable sales in underserved markets and have done so in ways that help build more vibrant and enduring communities. In the balance of the chapter, we both provide a guide to what your company as a whole needs to do to successfully grow your sales, as well as give specific "how-to's" for sales managers. These approaches will help you not only boost sales but also improve access to goods and services for people in underserved markets.

UNDERSTANDING THE MARKET CONTEXT

How does a company sustain growth when the market that it is selling into begins to reach saturation? How can your company continue to grow profitably when there are fewer and fewer new customers in your core markets?

It's easy to underestimate the opportunity for increased sales and profits in underserved communities. Most businesses have done so for years. After all, the people living in these communities are mostly poor, and poor people don't have much money. And if they don't have much money, they can't buy much. That means the underserved communities aren't a very attractive market, right?

Wrong. The key mistake here is to overlook the fact that there are billions of underserved consumers in domestic and overseas markets, and they often live in high-density neighborhoods. This means that the aggregate purchasing power of these consumers is enormous. Even though each individual may have a relatively small amount of money, as a group these markets are huge. In addition, although many of the individuals in such markets are poor, some of them are middle class, and a few are quite wealthy. The size of the markets means that even a modest percentage of middle-income consumers can translate into significant sales. To see this point, just remember that there are more middle-income consumers in China than in the entire United States. The heterogeneity of these markets can be a challenge for marketers—but it also can be a boon for sales, if you can crack the code on how to sell successfully.

Consider the following facts:

In the United States:

- The purchasing power of one demographic group—African Americans—in the United States alone, if aggregated, would constitute an economy bigger than Canada's. Recent estimates show that the total purchasing power of all ethnic minorities in the United States will top $1.5 trillion in 2009 (Humphreys, 2004).

- The 100 fastest-growing companies located in inner-city underserved markets in the United States recorded an average five-year growth rate of 716 percent as of 2005—a compound annual rate of 54 percent (Initiative for a Competitive Inner City, 2005).

- America's inner cities represent $85 billion in retail spending per year, approximately 7 percent of U.S. retail spending, larger than the formal retail market in Mexico (Initiative for a Competitive Inner City, 2004).

In the developing world:

- Urban low-income areas in the developing world offer highly concentrated purchasing power. For example, the low-income areas around Rio de Janeiro alone are estimated to have a total annual purchasing power of $1.2 billion (Prahalad and Hammond, 2004).

- Taken together, nine developing nations—China, India, Brazil, Mexico, Russia, Indonesia, Turkey, South Africa, and Thailand—have a combined gross domestic product (GDP) that is larger, in purchasing power parity, than the combined GDPs of Japan, Germany, France, the United Kingdom, and Italy (Prahalad and Hammond, 2004).

- Fully 500 million low-income individuals have enough income and assets to benefit from access to financial services, but only 25 million are being served today (Women's World Banking, 2005).

In tandem with these increased market opportunities, the barriers to entry into emerging markets are rapidly disappearing. In the United States, for example, concerns about crime and other inner-city deficits are declining. In fact, for over ten years Michael Porter, Harvard business professor and competitive strategy expert, has been extolling the competitive advantages of the inner city, which include: centrality and proximity to transportation nodes, availability of labor, and unmet local market demand. In developing countries, the business environment is also improving as a result of, among other factors, liberalized trade regimes, increased foreign direct investment, and the development of domestic financial markets.

Pursuing underserved markets is not new. Dramatic moves into what were formerly underserved markets have been done many times before: I.M. Singer (the sewing machine manufacturer) in the 19th century, Ford Motor Company in the 20th century, and CEMEX (the cement manufacturer) in the 21st century all understood that profitable growth can be achieved by democratizing the marketplace. The bold changes in production and marketing that let them sell into what were then underserved communities are what management experts Stuart Hart and Clayton Christensen call "disruptive innovation." This type of innovation dramatically changes the terms of competition. Hart and Christensen also point out the potential match between this type of innovation and the opportunities in underserved communities.

> The theory of disruptive innovation suggests that existing mainstream markets are the wrong place to look for major new waves of growth. . . . Developing countries are ideal target markets for disruptive technologies for at least two reasons. First, business models that are forged in low-income markets travel well; that is, they can be profitably applied in more places than models defined in high-income markets. In addition to having more adaptable business models, disruptive innovators also compete against nonconsumption—that is, they offer a product or service to people who would otherwise be left out entirely or poorly served by existing products. (Hart and Christensen, 2002)

Clearly, there are potentially enormous markets here. The question is how to tap them profitably. It's one thing to figure out how to profitably sell a computer to a family with a household income of $25,000; it's quite different to figure out how to sell one to a family with a household income of $1,000. The balance of this chapter explains how to employ the five success factors to address challenges like this one in sales and marketing. It also will show you how to do this in ways that create benefits for community as well as business.

UNLOCKING THE PROFIT POTENTIAL OF UNDERSERVED MARKETS

In this section, we go point by point through each success factor, explaining what's different about underserved markets and what to do about those differences.

■ I. MINE AND TRANSLATE LOCAL MARKET INFORMATION

What's Different about Underserved Markets

Every manager knows the importance of accurate, up-to-the minute information about his or her company's customers and competitors. Most companies invest millions of dollars each year in gathering this information through surveys, focus groups, point-of-sale information systems, and industry data. Many companies assume that they can use their current methods of gathering market information, and their current models and tools for analyzing information, to learn about and assess new opportunities in underserved markets. Most are wrong.

Why? Because underserved markets are not described accurately by many of the market information and analysis systems that are commonly used by businesses. There are two major ways in which standard market information and standard market analysis get the picture wrong:

- Methodologies for gathering data that work well for middle-income consumers don't work well for consumers in underserved markets. Businesses end up gathering the wrong information, or gathering it in ways that provide a skewed image of potential sales and profits in underserved communities.

- The market analysis models that businesses use to analyze the data

What's different?

- Standard data-gathering approaches don't work well.
- Analytic models fail to predict behavior in underserved markets.

What to do about it.

- Use information brokers to provide specialized information and analysis.
- Develop learning laboratories to test products, incentives, and marketing messages quickly and efficiently.

produce the right answers for middle-income consumers but don't accurately predict low-income consumer behavior.

Standard Data-gathering Approaches Don't Work Well

Most of the methods that companies use to gather market information are geared for current customers, who often are middle-income or above. They gather information and track indicators to judge demand and cost for middle-income consumers. But these approaches often don't give an accurate assessment of market demand and cost in underserved communities.

For example, many companies use income data to estimate purchasing potential. But research shows clearly that low-income consumers typically purchase much more (often as much as 30% more) than their income. This occurs in part because of cash they receive through the "informal" economy (i.e., payments not reported to any government authority). It also occurs through gifts, remittances, and transfer payments that are not captured in income data (Ford Foundation, 2005).

Even when companies use purchasing data, the translation from middle- to low-income neighborhoods may not be accurate. For example, consider national consumer purchasing surveys, which are often the bedrock on which many consumer market analyses rest. Because purchasing per household in underserved communities is relatively small, the national data sets often undersample these groups and so are inadequate predictors of the purchasing patterns and costs associated with consumers in underserved communities. In addition to the problem of sampling, underserved communities are often difficult to survey in cost-effective ways (via telephone, mail, and Internet). This is particularly true in developing countries.

Even getting an accurate count of the low-income population in a given market area can be difficult because official censuses tend to undercount low-income individuals. These individuals may not all be legally documented. They may not have permanent homes. They may be concerned that participating in a census will lead to potential problems with authorities. All these factors significantly hinder accurate counting of low-income consumers as compared with middle- and upper-income consumers.

A good example of the potential inadequacy of standard market information in assessing underserved markets is provided by the work of Social Compact, a nonprofit dedicated to providing better market information on inner-city communities in the United States. Social Compact has pioneered The Neighborhood Market Drill Down, a market analysis model built on innovative sources of dependable, business-oriented data to provide a more accurate picture of economic growth and purchasing power in underserved communities. The Drill Down adds alternative data sets to the standard market sets, and it supplements them with direct collection of primary source data in the markets. Alternative data sources include auto registrations, building permits, bill payment data, and property sales. See the box below for a more detailed list. The Drill Down analysis often shows hidden opportunities that standard information sources do not.

For example, when Social Compact analyzed the Columbia Heights community in Washington, D.C., its research showed that this market is far larger and growing much faster than standard

---

Management Tips: Finding Alternative Data Sets for Underserved Markets

Underserved markets require alternative data sources to assist in evaluating market size, buying power, market stability, and growth potential. Here are some potential data sources that you may want to consider in addition to the data you are currently using:

- bill payment data
- auto registration
- tax assessment
- school enrollment
- reported crimes
- property sales
- commercial credit
- housing values
- housing tenure (owner vs. renter occupied)
- residential building permits
- new construction

Source: Social Compact, 2005.

sources would suggest. The total population was 51.0 percent higher than the U.S. Census reported, and the rate of growth was 55.9 percent higher than that predicted by the U.S. Census. The difference in population size and growth were primarily a function of (1) multiple households residing within one residence, and (2) the huge influx of immigrants into the market; both populations are undercounted by standard approaches.

The Drill Down also found higher average annual household consumption than the Census did: $58,752 versus $43,606. This dramatic increase is due primarily to the inclusion of a cash economy projection that averages $10,000 per household in this market. Putting together the larger population and the greater consumption, The Drill Down found a much larger total market: $1.4 billion versus $851 million—an increase of 70.7 percent. Clearly, information gained from standard data-gathering approaches won't provide accurate answers as to whether and how to invest in approaching this market (Social Compact, 2004).

Analytic Models Don't Translate Well

Many businesses have developed complex analytic models to turn market information into knowledge managers can act on. These models help inform many decisions, from strategic choices about which markets to pursue, to product design and pricing, to distribution and store siting. Many of these models were developed for current customers and markets, and thus they do not translate well when applied to underserved communities.

For example, most retail companies build their analysis of the desirability of a specific location in part on the basis of median household income of the trade area surrounding that location. But for densely populated inner cities, research shows that concentrated buying power—income per acre or per square mile—provides a better indication of the total dollars available in a market for retail sales than does median household income. Indeed, the total purchasing power in an urban market is driven as much or more by density as it is by median income. Many suburbs, for example, have above-average median income but are sparsely populated relative to the city, so that fewer total consumer dollars are available. In many central cities, by contrast, population density more than makes up for median income, yielding much higher concentrated buying power. If you're interested in how many dollars are available to be spent at your store, be aware that data on median income can be downright misleading (Initiative for a Competitive Inner City, 2002).

Gathering accurate market information, and translating it accurately for your specific needs, can be challenging. But companies that have succeeded in underserved markets have found many ways of addressing these challenges—approaches that you can use successfully as well. In marketing and sales, the strategies can be distilled into two primary approaches:

- *Use information brokers*: experts who specialize in gathering and analyzing information about underserved communities. Companies use this expertise to design systems and models that work for their products and services in underserved markets.
- *Develop learning laboratories*: pilot programs with robust information-gathering components that enable a company to learn how to gauge market demand and costs in underserved markets while testing out a specific product or service.

What to Do in Underserved Markets

Use Information Brokers

Companies that have successfully entered underserved markets often use specialized information brokers, such as Social Compact (noted above). These brokers gather, analyze, and synthesize information from a wide variety of nonstandard sources to provide better insight into the buying power, purchasing habits, and interests of consumers in low-income markets. For example, information brokers focusing on inner-city neighborhoods in the United States track real-time variables such as changes in school enrollment, car registrations, and home renovation loans. These variables reflect up-to-the-minute changes in concentrated purchasing power and consumer preferences.

Information brokers also conduct customized research that enables them to better understand the specific purchasing patterns of low-income consumers. For example, the Initiative for an Inner City, one such broker, regularly conducts a survey focused on inner-city residents. The survey provides detailed information on the unique buying habits of inner-city consumers and allows retailers to compare them to the buying habits of consumers elsewhere. This type of information is highly useful to companies that want to customize their offerings for the inner-city market. It also benefits consumers, because it ensures that their needs and interests are communicated more accurately to the companies who serve their markets.

Develop Learning Laboratories

Many companies use pilot programs to test out new markets and new products. But the key to successfully developing and marketing new products in underserved markets is to move beyond pilot programs to "learning laboratories." These efforts marry pilot programs with rigorous data-gathering and analysis. You can think of pilot programs as trading expeditions heading into unknown territory: the map of the territory that the expedition brings back can sometimes be more valuable than the profits earned from the trading, but the expedition only brings back a map if it takes along someone who is responsible for gathering and analyzing the information and producing a map at the end.

Hewlett-Packard (HP) has used this approach to meet its goal of dramatically increasing its sales in the growing markets in underserved communities across the globe. In order to better understand the needs and interests of low-income consumers, as well as how to help strengthen the social and economic bases in emerging markets, HP has developed a half-dozen "i-communities" worldwide. In each one, HP created public-private partnerships to accelerate economic development through the application of technology while simultaneously opening new markets and developing new products and services for those markets.

The i-communities serve as living laboratories, helping HP understand how to provide services to low-income individuals and creating insights that are useful in other parts of HP's business. For example, in the i-community in Kuppam, India, HP pioneered a solar-powered, backpack-size digital camera and printer that has brought the convenience of photography to the Kuppam communities and created business opportunities for young entrepreneurs.

But this project did more than simply test the market for photography among members of a low-income population. It also provided valuable in-depth information about how photography is used in Indian society. The insights helped HP to better design digital photography products for middle-income users elsewhere in India as well. In digital photography and other products, the i-community activities complemented and supported the market research and development conducted by other parts of HP. In fact, HP has replicated the model and applied the market learnings in other emerging markets such as South Africa (Dunn and Yamashita, 2003; Partridge, 2003).

■ 2. ADAPT BUSINESS MODEL TO COMMUNITY REALITIES

What's Different about Underserved Markets

Global companies have been stunningly successful in adapting their products and services to local markets around the world. They have taken core sets of products and competencies and been able to deliver them profitably to market segments in six continents. As the ultimate example of global product standardization, consider the Internet—delivered to every user with exactly the same TCP/IP protocol.

And yet experience shows that this approach often fails when engaging customer segments in underserved markets, for two key reasons:

- *Consumer tradeoffs are different in underserved markets.* Consumers in every market segment make tradeoffs among convenience, quality, features, and cost. For some products, there are similar tradeoffs across the income scale. Consider McDonald's, which has done very well with nearly the same format in Beverly Hills and Harlem alike. However, there are other products in which tradeoffs differ significantly, making the mainstream product unattractive in underserved markets. This is particu-

---

What's different?

- Consumers in underserved markets make different trade-offs in convenience, quality, features, and cost.
- Unit costs are often higher in underserved markets.

What to do about it.

- Reconfigure product features, price points, and format.
- Develop new distribution channels rooted in the community.
- Use "leapfrogging technology" to cut out elements of the cost structure.

---

larly true for consumer products with a high price per unit.

- *Unit costs are often higher in underserved markets.* Customers in underserved markets often buy in smaller quantities, are less connected to the mainstream media, and live in more isolated communities. When companies' marketing and distribution strategies aim to reach these populations in standard ways, these factors can drive up the cost per unit, making the customers less desirable financially.

What to Do in Underserved Markets

Companies have addressed these challenges by reinventing their products and services in a new form for underserved markets, by developing new distribution channels with businesses and institutions rooted in the community, and by deploying leapfrogging technology to help drive down the cost of reaching customers.

Reconfigure Product Features, Price Points, and Format in New Form

Products that are appropriate for middle- and upper-income consumers often need to be entirely reinvented for low-income consumers. Companies need to understand in depth the specific tradeoffs and requirements of low-income consumers, and redesign their products and services for those consumers' needs.

Hindustan Lever's reinvention of its mainline detergent product into a new form—Wheel detergent—provides a good example. In order to meet the needs of low-income consumers in certain areas in India, Hindustan Lever formulated Wheel to substantially reduce the ratio of oil to water in the product, responding to the fact that poor populations often wash their clothes in rivers and other public water systems. Hindustan Lever created packaging for Wheel in single-use sachets. The company also changed the cost structure of its detergent business so it could profitably sell Wheel at a lower price point than its other detergents. Wheel was quickly embraced by the consumers in underserved markets, helping Hindustan Lever to attain a 38 percent share of the detergent market across India (Prahalad, 2004). This gave consumers a product that worked well for them and also reduced the environmental impact.

Repackaging the product for single-use servings, as Hindustan Lever did for Wheel, is an example of a situation where a company responded to consumers in an underserved market who make significantly different tradeoffs from those of middle-income consumers. The low-income consumers value the low total cost, the small space requirements, and the convenience of the single-use sachet, even though the cost per use for single sachets is typically higher than that for the same products sold in larger bottles and cans. As a result, the demand for products sold in single-use packets in low-income markets has been growing rapidly. For example, in the market for shampoo in India, single-use sachets grew from 49 percent to 60 percent of the total shampoo market, by value, from 1998 to 2002 (Prahalad, 2004).

To achieve a high volume of profitable sales in ethnic urban markets in the United States, supermarket chains such as Shaw's and Pathmark have changed their store format, merchandising, price points, loss leaders, and overall store ambience. For organizations in which the standard store formats and merchandising have been honed down to successful models from one suburban store to the next, the need to dramatically reinvent the store format can pose challenges. But the profits and sales can be attractive enough to make the hard work of reinventing the format worth the effort. It also creates a store that better meets the needs and interests of underserved consumers.

Shaw's Supermarket in New Haven, Connecticut, is a good example. Shaw's management was attracted to the site initially because market studies showed a high level of unmet demand. There was no major supermarket within two miles, and only 20 percent of the area's residents owned cars. Shaw's would capture a large share of the food spending if the company could get the residents into the store and provide them with an attractive array of products.

But Shaw's management also knew that getting the residents into the store, and finding the right mix of products, would not be easy. The store would need to draw individuals from a wide cross-section of ethnic and income backgrounds. The store was located in a low-income neighborhood whose residents were primarily African American. In order to succeed, however, the store would also need to draw in students and employees from Yale University, whose campus began several blocks away. In addition, within the two-mile trade area, New Haven was home to a dizzying array of ethnic groups. The Shaw's market team identified 42 different ethnic and religious affiliations within the trade area. Clearly, a "one size fits all" model wouldn't work.

To develop the right product mix, Shaw's management collaborated with community groups and organized meetings with the ethnic leadership to discuss product offerings. Meeting in a former YWCA, Shaw's buyers and category managers, sitting at tables arranged by category (e.g., produce, seafood), conversed one-on-one with the community representatives and solicited ideas on what products to carry. From this dialogue, the company customized its merchandising approach to fit the community's ethnic mix. As an example, the store chose to stock fresh goat meat to satisfy the needs of consumers from some Caribbean countries.

Thanks to target merchandising and marketing, the store has also been successful at drawing members of the Yale community. Each year, Shaw's prepares a gift pack for new Yale students containing toothpaste, mouthwash, soap, and a redeemable phone card. Last year, Shaw's distributed 500 gift packs during freshman orientation week.

By reinventing the product format, merchandising, and marketing strategies, Shaw's has been able to create a profitable store and to bring high-quality, competitively priced merchandise to an underserved community that formerly had no easy access to a supermarket (Initiative for a Competitive Inner City, 2002).

Develop New Distribution Channels Rooted in the Community

Companies often find that distribution systems and marketing approaches that work well for middle- and upper-income consumers are not appropriate or cost effective for low-income consumers.

One successful approach to lowering the costs of distribution and marketing is to partner with businesses or local organizations that already provide goods and services to the target customer group. These partnerships enable the corporation to reach the customers in a more cost-effective way by cutting marketing and distribution costs.

In India, for instance, Arvind Mills has introduced an entirely new delivery system for blue jeans. Arvind, the world's fifth-largest denim manufacturer, found Indian domestic denim sales limited. At $40 to $60 a pair, the jeans were not affordable to the masses, and the existing distribution system reached only a few towns and villages. So Arvind introduced "Ruf n Tuf" jeans—a ready-to-make kit of jeans components (denim, zipper, rivets, and a patch) priced at about $6. Kits were distributed through a network of thousands of local tailors, many in small rural towns and villages, whose self-interest motivated them to market the kits extensively. Ruf n Tuf jeans are now the largest-selling jeans in India, easily surpassing Levi's and other brands from the United States and Europe (Prahalad and Hart, 2002).

Deploy Leapfrogging Technology to Lower Costs

Companies selling well to underserved markets often deploy leapfrogging technology—technology that enables them to cut out expensive elements of their cost structure by leapfrogging over an existing segment of the cost structure. This innovative move enables them to generate attractive margins, even at the lower price points common in these markets.

For example, in South Africa, Standard Bank has aggressively pursued leapfrogging technology to lower costs in serving low-income customers. With 6 million accounts and total assets of R395b ($48.8 billion), Standard Bank is South Africa's second-largest bank overall and its largest retail bank. In 1999, Standard Bank launched "E Plan," an account that employs ATM technologies to lower the account cost structure and serve clients who could not be served profitably under the bank's standard operation—and therefore who could not access the bank's services. E Plan offers a combination of account features geared to meet the financial needs of low-income consumers, it has a fee structure that encourages electronic-only transactions, and it focuses on simplicity in its processes and convenience in its locations. These features have helped to eliminate teller transactions, which are ten times more costly than ATM transactions, and to reduce customer support requirements. The program's scale indicates that E Plan has proven an effective way to draw low-income people into banking: in a country with a working population of 11 million, 3.1 million accounts were opened by the end of 2004, with a growth rate of 12 percent from 2003 to 2004. E Plan has not only created a profitable market for banking, but it also has brought individuals in underserved communities the benefits of retail banking—a safe way to save, a secure way to pay bills, and the creation of a financial history, which is important for the individuals' future opportunities (Lobenhofer, Bredenkamp, and Stegman, 2003; Standard Bank, 2006).

In the United States, Rush Communications used smart card technology and new database technology for tracking and managing stored value card transactions to create the RushCard. This stored value card enables holders to make purchases over the Internet or at point of sale terminals even if they have no bank accounts and regardless of their credit history. Using leapfrogging technology, Rush Communications was able to lower the cost of issuing and managing the card transactions to the point where it could deliver the card at an attractive price point and still make a profit. The process of developing this innovative product is profiled in Chapter 4. As of the end of 2005, Rush Communications had approximately 500,000 customers who use the RushCard, creating not only a profitable line of business for the company but also access to Internet commerce and greater security in financial transactions for individuals from underserved communities.

■ 3. CHANGE INTERNAL INCENTIVES AND CHALLENGE CULTURAL ASSUMPTIONS

What's Different in Underserved Markets

The diversity and cultural richness of underserved communities can be part of their market potential. But these features can also create challenges that companies need to address in both organizational structure and culture. In most companies, structure follows strategy: the existing organizational structure was developed to support the core strategy, or corporate culture, of the company. Reporting relationships, compensation structures, and communication flows are typically set up to enable and motivate staff to focus on existing markets and customers. In many cases, companies have found that the existing organizational structures and incentives simply don't work well when focusing on underserved markets.

> **What's different?**
>
> - Organizational structure designed for mainstream doesn't work well for underserved markets.
> - Company assumptions about consumers in underserved markets are inaccurate.
>
> **What to do about it.**
>
> - Align incentives and communication in ways that support sales in low-income markets.
> - Challenge cultural assumptions and biases.

Such was the case for a major U.S. bank that had decided to pursue the market for homeownership mortgages among low-income individuals. Even though the product was well designed, had an attractive pricing structure, and was well received in market testing, the product roll-out initially did poorly. The problem? The existing performance incentive for the loan originators wasn't aligned with the new product. When the product was launched, the loan originators were provided with a performance incentive that was based on the total dollar volume of loans they originated. The loans to low-income individuals typically had a lower principal amount than loans to middle-income individuals. But even though the loan principal was lower, the amount of work required to originate and close the loan was about the same as that for loans to middle-income individuals. As a result, the loan originators tended to focus more on generating loans for middle-income individuals than for lower-income individuals. Even though the margins were attractive to the bank, the incentive for the origination staff was not aligned properly. Once the bank shifted the incentive to be based on the total number of loans originated, rather than on the total dollar volume of loans originated, the originations took off and the loan product became one of the major lines of business for the bank. This enabled many consumers from underserved communities to get home loans at attractive rates, and thus be able to afford to buy their own homes.

What to Do in Underserved Markets

Adapt Organizational Structure to Realities in Underserved Markets

Research by the Center for Corporate Citizenship at Boston College (Rochlin and Boguslaw, 2001) shows that companies use three key approaches to adapt their organizational structures so that they can compete successfully in underserved markets: (1) coordinate activities across the business, (2) assign appropriate responsibility for implementation, and (3) create functional accountability and incentives that reach across business functions.

1. *Coordinate Activities Across the Business.* Reaching underserved markets often requires companies to leverage and coordinate core competencies across functions. For example, Safeco, a leading insurance company, wanted to expand sales in low-income neighborhoods across the United States. It recognized that successfully marketing its insurance products in inner-city neighborhoods would require coordinating activities across a broad span of business units, including public relations, claims, underwriting, administration, human resources, legal, marketing, regional management, and small business insurance. To accomplish this coordination it created the Diversity Marketing Committee, which meets seven times a year to identify how the functions of each department can work to leverage the others. For example, this committee has changed the process for determining where to locate a new sales office. Prior to the creation of this committee, when Safeco was considering where to open a new sales office, the administration unit would make the determination by itself primarily based on an analysis of cost-effective ways to cover a particular territory. Now, the committee staff reviews with Human Resources, Sales, and other units how opening an office in an urban setting can help with improving sales, enabling better recruitment of staff, and helping to improve the neighborhoods in which Safeco sells insurance.

2. *Assign Appropriate Responsibility for Implementation.* Clear responsibility for the marketing and implementation of a product or service for the underserved market is critical for success. Some companies have a particular manager responsible for overseeing all activities in pursuing an underserved market. At Texas Instruments, the responsibility for driving the coordinated effort to pursue a new market rests with the Minority/Women Business Development Manager. Other companies embed the responsibility in a cross-functional team. At JPMorgan Chase, the responsibility is managed by a cross-functional team, the Community Development Group. This group utilizes community development initiatives to incorporate and implement new products and services targeted toward underserved communities as well as mainstream ones. Both strategies have been successful as of evaluations through 2004.

3. *Create Functional Accountability and Incentives That Reach Across Business Functions.* The requirement to work across functions raises the challenge of managing accountability and incentives across functions. Accountabilities are often internal (goals and metrics that are managed and tracked within the company) as well as external (goals and metrics that are reported to the community). Most companies find it important to create clear quantitative goals for performance across teams and to provide complementary incentives to staff. (The incentives that Texas Instruments created for its cross-functional team noted in Chapter 3 is a good example.) It also is critically important to make sure that the existing incentive structures do not inhibit staff from focusing on underserved markets. The bank example cited in this chapter shows the need to remove or revise existing incentives structures when they inhibit staff from focusing on underserved markets.

Challenge Implicit Cultural Assumptions and Racial Biases

Strategies to engage underserved communities can run afoul of cultural assumptions and of racial, ethnic, and social biases. Experience has shown that managers sometimes misperceive the risks and rewards of engaging with underserved communities, particularly when the managers themselves have limited direct personal experience with those communities. They also hold—though often do not consciously articulate—racial, ethnic, and social assumptions about members of the underserved communities.

When these assumptions are faulty, they can lead to a range of consequences, from a simple misunderstanding of customers in underserved markets, all the way to outright racial and ethnic discrimination. For example, a number of major U.S. insurance companies made multimillion dollar settlements in court cases over the past ten years because of damning evidence of discrimination in their operations. In several cases, the courts found that pairs of shoppers, identical in every respect except race, were given significantly different policies and prices by the insurance agents. There are similar cases showing that automobile sales staff gave larger price discounts to white men than to black women. These findings are deeply troubling from the perspective of a society seeking just and equal treatment for all its members. They also pose major barriers for businesses seeking to enter low-income markets.

Companies that have successfully entered low-income markets often work to identify and change cultural and racial biases within the organization that prevent their managers from understanding and developing opportunities in those markets. The core of their strategies often involves making these assumptions explicit, so that they can be addressed and managed. Another key element of their strategies is to engage managers with the communities, and the communities with managers through projects, volunteer work, and mentoring activities, so that each side can gain firsthand understanding of the other.

JPMorgan Chase has found a way to identify and address cultural challenges that not only improves the company's external relationships with target communities but also embeds a cultural awareness within the business itself. JPMorgan Chase began to increase its focus on creating services for low- to moderate-income populations in the late 1990s, both in response to pressures for increased lending volume and as a result of regulatory pressure for greater services in low-income neighborhoods. The company offered more affordable loans and eliminated ATM fees in urban neighborhoods to better serve potential customers there. But it also worked to better align its organization and corporate culture with potential customers. From the beginning of the process, the company emphasized the importance of strategic partnering with community members and groups to best understand its new target market.

To attain this goal, the company has created the position of "StreetBanker." These employees, formerly community relations officers, are charged with linking community leaders, nonprofit organizations, and governmental agencies to lending businesses at JPMorgan Chase. Their tasks include identifying and understanding community needs, responding to community concerns about banking services, communicating those concerns to the company, and making connections between community groups and Chase business units. Through these activities, StreetBankers make a connection between the community's needs and Chase's services and products. Their role helps the company as a whole, and lenders in particular, to understand the needs and expectations of low-income customers and to develop and deliver lending products and approaches that meet those needs.

On the lending side of JPMorgan Chase's business, relationship managers work to develop business opportunities and create relationships within their assigned areas, including low-income communities. The work of StreetBankers informs this function by identifying the important issues and paving the way for potential relationships by gathering information and building trust.

JPMorgan Chase has grasped the importance of understanding the culture of the communities it hopes to serve with new and traditional banking products. The creation of internal positions such as StreetBankers helps the company to gather the most accurate information about needs and opportunities in underserved communities and to communicate that effectively to loan officers at the bank. (Rochlin and Boguslaw, 2001).

Another approach to gaining a more accurate understanding of underserved markets is to hire and promote individuals who reflect the racial and ethnic composition of those markets. Many corporations have developed policies for identifying, training, and promoting qualified individuals from these communities. This is both a matter of social justice and an important way to help the company better understand the market and increase its sales. There are many examples: programs by insurance companies to recruit an ethnically diverse network of insurance agents, and efforts by hospitality and fast food companies to develop ethnically diverse management for restaurants and hotels located in underserved communities. Strategies for successfully retaining and promoting an ethnically diverse workforce are discussed in more detail in Chapter 2.

■ 4. CREATE PARTNERSHIPS AND STRATEGIC ALLIANCES

What's Different in Underserved Markets

In many underserved markets, there are market barriers that prevent companies from achieving profitable sales when working through their normal business networks. In addition, corporations can face considerable distrust from residents of underserved communities, which reduces demand and increases scrutiny by community-elected officials and regulators. Creating partnerships and strategic alliances can help address both challenges.

What to Do in Underserved Markets

Build Partnerships to Help Overcome Market Barriers

There are three common examples of market barriers. One example occurs when the cost structure for delivering the product through normal distribution channels creates a price point that is too high for the market. The second occurs when there isn't an effective means to aggregate and channel demand, making the cost to acquire customers too high. The third occurs when there are political or bureaucratic obstacles to market entry.

Partnerships can play a wide range of roles in helping businesses to overcome market barriers. They can bring new knowledge, skill, resources, and connections to the business networks. They can assist businesses to reduce the costs of reaching and serving their

> **What's different?**
>
> - Market barriers prevent profitable sales.
> - Distrust of corporations reduces demand, and increases regulation.
>
> **What to do about it.**
>
> - Build partnerships to lower costs, increase sales, and reduce regulatory difficulties.
> - Build trust by helping underserved communities to increase income and assets.

customers. They can help to improve markets and increase demand for products and services. Finally, they can help to build community support for business growth and make it easier to get the regulatory approvals required.

1. *Reduce Costs.* Partnerships are often focused on reducing the cost to identify, attract, and serve low-income customers. Because low-income consumers typically require a lower price point, driving down costs becomes a critical success factor. While many of these partnerships are between a single corporation and one or more local partners, some involve multiple corporations. One example is the Loss Prevention Partnership Program. It was created in 1999 by a coalition of insurers, including State Farm, Travelers Property Casualty, and Prudential, together with Neighborhood Reinvestment (a national nonprofit organization focused on increasing homeownership). In 2004, Travelers Property Casualty merged with St. Paul Companies to form St. Paul Travelers.

The Loss Prevention Partnership Program sought to create mutual benefits for both insurers and low-income homeowners in urban neighborhoods. It had three key components: homeowner education about safety hazards, free home safety assessments, and a low-interest loan fund. This fund enabled low-income homeowners to repair hazardous conditions discovered during the home safety assessment. The program was piloted from 2000 to 2003 in six cities across the United States. In this three-year period, the program educated more than 6,000 individuals in home safety seminars, conducted more than 1,300 home safety evaluations, and loaned more than $2.5 million for home safety. As an added benefit, once consumers became educated about home safety, some emerged to provide leadership for neighborhood crime prevention and to address other obstacles that have traditionally made communities less insurable. Initial evaluations show that this program both (1) enables the insurance companies to increase the profitable sale of homeownership insurance in these neighborhoods, and (2) improves the safety and security of residents' homes. The coalition of insurers expanded the program to 25 cities in 2004–2005 (Weiser and Zadek, 2000; Pittman, 2004a; Pittman, 2004b; Green, 2004).

2. *Aggregate Demand to Increase Sales.* Partnerships help to create an effective market by aggregating demand. For example, Working Today, a national nonprofit in the United States, focuses on the market for health insurance, life insurance, and disability insurance among freelance workers in the United States, many of whom are low-income. The existing insurance market cannot provide this type of insurance to freelance workers at an attractive rate, due to what is termed "adverse selection." Adverse selection refers to the fact that when insurance is sold to individuals (rather than groups), the younger, healthier individuals are much less likely to buy health insurance than older, less healthy individuals. This dramatically increases the cost of providing insurance to this group. In 2001, Working Today launched the Portable Benefits Network, which is a method of working with professional associations, membership- and community-based organizations, unions, and companies that employ many freelancers to aggregate demand across large numbers of freelance workers. This move both lowers the cost of marketing and ameliorates the issue of adverse selection. The move has increased profitable sales of health insurance while at the same time enabling freelancers to purchase affordable health insurance through the Network.

Working Today is now partnering with a range of insurance companies, who are able to work through it to provide insurance products and services on a cost-effective basis to these workers. As of 2004, its Portable Benefits network was serving 16,000 individuals in New York City, and expanding rapidly (Working Today, 2004).

3. *Build Community Support and Reduce Regulatory Difficulties.* Corporations are often not welcomed or trusted in underserved communities, even though they may be bringing higher-quality goods and services at more attractive prices. Local opposition may come from a lack of understanding or trust, or it may be driven by the existing businesses in the market, who rightly understand that being exposed to national and international competition will not necessarily help them thrive. Even though the businesses that are coming in will provide goods and services on terms that are better for the consumers, the local businesses may still rally support to

keep them out. The cautionary tale of Pathmark's expansion into Harlem (see Introduction) provides a good example.

Many businesses develop local partners to help build community support and navigate the complexities of local politics. They may also rely on local partners to help move more expeditiously through the permitting and regulatory processes. Supermarket developers in the United States frequently partner with local Community Development Corporations (CDCs), who can help them get their projects completed more quickly. For example, when Shaw's sought to build a new supermarket in inner-city New Haven (see page 27), it worked with the Great Dwight Development Corporation, a local CDC. The CDC helped to ensure that the community supported the project. It worked closely with Shaw's and the City of New Haven to ensure that local residents would be trained and ready for the jobs when the supermarket opened, and that Shaw's would give preference to local residents in hiring. It also worked to move the Shaw's process through the complex thicket of zoning and regulatory issues that were involved in building a supermarket-anchored shopping center in a densely populated neighborhood. The end result saw the creation of more jobs in the neighborhood and a reduction in grocery costs of 30 to 50 percent from the small convenience stores that had served the neighborhood previously (Masterson, 2001).

Home Group Ltd., a U.K. social landlord company and provider of affordable rented housing, provides another example with its work in the North Benwell area of Britain. The area experienced many economic and social disturbances in the 1990s. Community organizations and the local governments subsequently sought to rejuvenate the community with selective demolition, capital works, and environmental improvements. However, these initiatives did not address the factors underlying the low demand for housing in North Benwell, a problem that was detrimental to Home Group Ltd.'s opportunities in the area.

To increase the demand for housing, in both sale and rental markets, the company partnered with civic organizations, such as the local police force and youth organizations, to create the North Benwell Neighbourhood Management Initiative (NBNMI). The company is the lead partner in this initiative. Its objectives include (1) stabilizing the local housing market, (2) reducing the number of empty properties, and (3) improving the local urban environment.

The impact of the NBNMI has been felt both in the community and at Home Group Ltd. Crime rates have dropped in the neighborhood, and neighborhood aesthetics have improved, increasing North Benwell's desirability as a residential area. One example of a quick fix was the company's decision to install colorful window boards in abandoned properties to enhance appearance and signify hope to possible new tenants. As a result of the initiative, the area is experiencing an increased housing demand to the point that there are waiting lists of families anticipating a move to the community. Home Group Ltd. has responded to the increase by renovating some of its own long-empty properties to be more attractive to potential renters. The company's long-term goal is to eventually sell many of these properties to ensure that the community's new residents become less transient, creating a more stable environment (Business in the Community, 2005).

Build Trust by Helping Underserved Communities to Increase Income and Assets

Large corporations often face a lack of trust on the part of many consumers and residents of underserved communities. After all, many of these individuals have had bad experiences with large corporations—turned down by loan officers, treated poorly by service staff, provided with inadequate care and attention, or seen jobs disappear from communities as facilities close down. Residents of underserved communities may also feel that the "balance of trade" with large corporations is entirely one-sided, with the corporations selling high-priced products to the communities' residents and extracting value without providing benefits to those communities in return. For example, Nike has received considerable criticism for selling sneakers at $100 apiece to youth in underserved communities in the United States. Similarly, the book *World on Fire* documents how increasing global trade in the developing world without attending to benefits within the communities can lead to ethnic hatred and political instability between the haves and the have-nots (Chua, 2004).

To ensure sales that endure over time, as well as to establish a socially responsible presence in the community, it is important for corporations both to be "neighbors of choice" and to be viewed as such by residents. If residents of a low-income community look critically at your company's relationship with their community and have the strong impression that "you get the gold mine and they get the shaft," you will likely face a rocky and combative relationship with the community over time. Fortunately, there are many effective strategies for improving the economic parity in the relationship. Core to all of these is to help underserved communities to increase their income and assets over time. The following four strategies have been used widely to achieve this result.

1. *Use Local Distributors.* This strategy is often employed by companies seeking to sell into underserved markets. It can lower distribution costs and increase acceptance by local consumers. It also helps to build income and assets when members of the community own and operate the local distributor businesses. For example, Hindustan Lever chose to retail its Wheel detergent through the thousands of small, locally owned rural stores where low-income consumers shop. In the United States, the Harbor Bank of Maryland partnered with Stop, Shop and Save, one of the largest minority-owned supermarket chains on the East Coast, to place Harbor Bank ATMs in Stop, Shop and Save markets around the Baltimore area. The new locations offered Harbor Bank the advantage of increasing its visibility by (1) positioning ATMs in locations where the bank did not have branches, and (2) providing a new revenue stream from non-customer ATM transaction fees. In addition to the ATMs achieving profitability, Harbor Bank has gained new customers in the community and increased revenue from ATM fees by about 20 percent. Through the partnership, Stop, Shop and Save can now compete more effectively with larger chains that offer ATM/banking services in their stores. The ATM machines also help generate additional foot traffic in the markets. Based on the success of this partnership, Harbor Bank is currently expanding ATM placement into inner-city convenience stores and food service outlets (WinWinPartner.com, 2004).

2. *Purchase from Local Suppliers.* This approach works very successfully in the United States and elsewhere for companies selling

goods into low-income and ethnic markets. Sometimes labeled "diversity purchasing" in the United States, companies make targeted efforts to increase their purchases from sources within low-income and ethnic communities. There has been a remarkable increase in growth of sales from diverse suppliers to major corporations in the United States over the past twenty-five years. The National Minority Supplier Development Council, which helps connect minority suppliers to major corporations, has data showing that sales from its members to major corporations grew from $1.0 billion in 1977 to $80.2 billion in 2003 (National Minority Supplier Development Council, 2005).

Companies purchase from these suppliers, first and foremost, because they offer quality products at competitive prices. But the suppliers also can help the purchasing companies to innovate products and services. As Arthur Martinez, CEO of Sears, noted in an interview, "By maintaining a large pool of potential vendors, a company widens its scope of innovative ideas, methods and markets. Minority vendors enhance those capabilities by providing valuable, culturally specific opportunities to help create new markets. In many cases, minority entrepreneurs identify lucrative markets long before mainstream companies make the same discoveries" (Weiser and Zadek, 2000). We explore strategies for purchasing from local suppliers in more detail in Chapter 4.

3. *Hire from Local Communities.* This approach can be attractive to businesses that have plants or stores located in or near underserved communities. As noted in the Pathmark and Shaw's examples, hiring from the local community was an important factor in creating a win-win relationship with the community. We review this approach in depth in Chapter 2.

4. *Invest in Local Infrastructure.* Companies can participate as partners in the community by investing in local institutions and infrastructure. This effort can range widely, from investments in schools and training, to hospitals and health care, to roads and ports. The most successful investments have two characteristics: (1) they are directly responsive to the expressed needs of the community, and (2) they represent a clear "win-win" proposition for both the businesses and the communities. The investment not only improves

the community's assets but also creates a long-term benefit for the company. GE's commitment to improving high schools in the communities in which its plants are located exemplifies this mutually beneficial approach. Improving high school performance helps promote life-long success for community residents and makes the communities more attractive as places to live and work. It also supports GE's need for a well-trained and skilled workforce for its plants (Committee to Encourage Corporate Philanthropy, 2005).

This section shows the wide range of roles that partnerships and alliances can play, and the types of benefits that they can bring to business and community alike. With this extensive a range, it is not surprising that corporate-community partnerships often figure in success stories. In fact, more than two-thirds of the companies in our research sample had formed a partnership with an organization in the community. These partnerships were with a wide range of organizations, including other businesses, government agencies, nonprofit organizations, and community groups.

The standard factors for success in partnerships across the business world also apply to partnerships for serving the underserved markets: clear goals, mutual needs, appropriate resources, well-structured governance, and high levels of communication. In Chapter 5, we explore in more detail the do's and don'ts of starting and maintaining a partnership.

■ 5. IMPROVE THE ENABLING ENVIRONMENT

What's Different in Underserved Markets

Surely some skeptics will say, "You've made what appears to be a good case for how a company can adapt its business practices to succeed in underserved markets. But this just means you don't really know what it's like to work in these communities. The enabling environment—laws, regulations, infrastructure, institutions—is very challenging and makes operating efficiently at scale nearly impossible." As so often is the case with skeptical comments, there is a grain of truth here. Especially in developing economies, the enabling environment often can and does pose impediments to increased sales in

What's different?

- Enabling environment—laws, regulations, infrastructure, and institutions— makes it difficult to operate efficiently.

What to do about it.

- Improve the quality of the infrastructure.
- Raise the bar for corporate behavior.
- Increase financial incentives for reaching consumers in underserved markets.

underserved communities. There are basic issues such as whether or not there is a rule of law, political stability, a functioning court system, and a security force controlled by the state. There can be complex issues such as whether the infrastructure required for distribution (roads, ports, telephone lines, Internet access, etc.) is in place and functioning well. Finally, there can be overarching issues such as how regulations enable or impede sales to specific customer groups.

In order to succeed in these markets, it is often necessary to work to change the enabling environment. This most often involves recruiting business and nonprofit allies to work together in coalitions to change the laws, regulations, infrastructure, and institutions that prevent entry into the underserved markets. Although there are a myriad of ways in which companies work to change the enabling environment, we can identify three broad types of strategies: (1) improve the quality of the infrastructure, (2) raise the bar for corporate behavior, and (3) increase financial incentives for reaching consumers in underserved markets.

What to Do in Underserved Markets

Improve the Quality of the Infrastructure

Especially in developing economies, companies often spend considerable effort helping to develop basic infrastructure such as the rule of law, political stability, a functioning court system, and a security force controlled by the state. Efforts can also support the development of a communications infrastructure and workforce skills. In addressing these issues, companies often work together collectively with other companies and with multilateral and bilateral institutions such as the World Bank.

Cisco's Networking Academy program is a good example of a company's effort to improve the enabling environment in a way that both creates value for communities and helps Cisco to place more of its products in underserved communities. The Cisco Networking Academy program is a comprehensive e-learning program that provides students with Internet technology skills. The Networking Academy delivers Web-based content, online assessment, student performance tracking, hands-on labs, instructor training and support, and preparation for industry standard certifications. With the skills they have learned, students can enter the workforce and get a well-paying job, or go on to more advanced studies.

Launched in October 1997 with 64 educational institutions in 7 states in the United States, the Networking Academy has spread to more than 150 countries. Since its inception, over 1.6 million students have enrolled at more than 10,000 Academies located in high schools, technical schools, colleges, universities, and community-based organizations.

Cisco's partners from business, government, and community organizations form a network that delivers the range of services and support needed to prepare students for tomorrow's jobs. Initially created to prepare students for the Cisco Certified Network Associate (CCNA) and Cisco Certified Network Professional (CCNP) degrees, the Academy curriculum has expanded. Optional courses include HP IT Essentials: PC Hardware and Software, and HP IT Essentials: Network Operating Systems (sponsored by Hewlett-Packard); and Panduit Network Infrastructure Essentials (sponsored by Panduit Corporation).

The program can be delivered in any location that has Internet access. With the United Nations Development Program, the United States Agency for International Development, and the International Telecommunication Union, Cisco has made the Academy program available to students in least developed countries such as Chad, Cambodia, Nigeria, Senegal, and Nepal.

The program creates value in underserved communities because it provides individuals with the skills they need to get a good job with family-supporting wages and benefits. It also helps the communities to have the workforce required to be able to expand Internet communications locally. Because Cisco's products form the core of a local or wide-area Internet network, the program also creates value for Cisco and helps it to sell its products (Cisco Systems, 2005).

Raise the Bar for Corporate Behavior

Companies that seek to reach low-income markets sometimes find that engaging with communities creates costs for them but not for their competitors, while the benefits accrue to everyone in the industry. This is the classic "free rider" problem, where some participants in the market take advantage of benefits created by the investments of other market actors without sharing in the cost of those investments. To address this problem, companies pursue strategies to build consensus and catalyze collective action within the business community in order to change public policy or create voluntary industry norms or standards. This raises the bar for all participants in the market.

One example from the world of project finance is the Equator Principles, a voluntary standard developed through work by non-profits and banks. These principles, were launched by 10 of the world's largest banks, and they have been joined by many others. The signatory banks provided 80 percent of the world's project finance as of 2005, and include banks such as Citibank, JPMorgan Chase, Barclay's, and ABN Amro. The principles require the signatories to adhere to social and environmental impact studies before providing financing to a project in developing markets. Many of the projects being financed are bridges, dams, roads, and airports, which are critical elements of the infrastructure required for economic development. Developed countries often have in place laws that require environmental and social impact analysis before undertaking these kinds of projects, but such laws are less common in developing countries. Creating a voluntary standard that banks agree to follow is an advantage for the banks because it removes the competitive disadvantage of any given bank being the only one that requires environmental and social impact analyses before lending. The standard is also an advantage for communities because now all projects that receive financing from multinational lenders will be required to consider environmental and social impacts before being started.

Increase Financial Incentives for Reaching Consumers

In some situations, corporations cannot provide certain products or services to communities because the cost of producing the product or the risks associated with providing the product are simply too high relative to the revenues that community members can afford to pay. One method of addressing this problem is to work with the public sector to change the financial incentives for community engagement. For example, the expense of providing housing for low-income individuals that meets accepted community standards often results in higher costs than most low-income individuals can afford. In the United States, the public sector often plays a role in providing subsidy funding for the gap between market costs and low-income pocketbooks, enabling the creation of a viable new market. One example of this has been the Low Income Housing Tax Credit, which enables the private sector in the United States to invest approximately \$12 billion per year in affordable housing. The tax credit essentially provides a subsidy from the government, through the tax system, to companies that invest in housing that is affordable to low-income individuals. The process opens up significant capital flows that would otherwise not be available. This leads to benefits for low income consumers because more affordable housing is built that they can rent or buy (Kahane, 2004).

MEASURING PROGRESS

What measures can help you track and manage your company's progress in sales and marketing to underserved communities? First let's consider the wide range of measures used by managers in sales and marketing to gauge the effectiveness of different ways of promoting sales and positioning the company and its brands in mainstream markets.

Although you are probably familiar with most measures, it may be helpful to take a minute to review some typical ones. The basic measures focus on sales revenue. Beyond the most basic measure—sales per period—managers typically try to get measures of consumers as they move through the sales cycle: awareness of product, interest in product, propensity to try or purchase product, first-time purchases, repeat sales/customer loyalty, recommendations of product to friends and colleagues, and customer defections. These measures go beyond the basic sales number to help managers understand and influence the dynamic that will lead to tomorrow's sales.

To plan marketing and better predict future sales, managers also typically develop customer segments, dividing up the population by demographics (age, income, and location) or psychographics (interests, affiliations, and self-perception). These segments respond differently to different product features, distribution channels, and promotions. Managers measure the effectiveness of promotion and advertising, looking at the number of impressions generated per customer segment and the impact on awareness and intention to purchase.

The capstone of sales measurement is the analysis of brand and image. What is the brand promise? How aware are the various customer segments of the brand promise? Has the company developed substantial brand equity—the enviable position in which a customer will pay more for a particular product because it bears the company's brand?

Most of these measures would apply as well to sales in underserved markets. What's typically different is the way in which the information is gathered. Because sales in these markets can involve lower margins, it is important that the method of tracking sales, customers, and channels be as efficient and low-cost as possible. This sometimes requires a high-tech approach, with each product bar-coded and scanned into an information system that ties together the whole enterprise. It sometimes requires a much lower-tech approach, particularly when the sales are occurring in very poor communities with limited infrastructure. In this case, it may be as simple as tracking how often the warehouse ships out a new delivery of Ruf n Tuf kits to the tailors (see page 29), who make the sales out in the villages and farms and who definitely do not have the ability to scan a barcode at the point of sale.

There is one unique aspect of sales to underserved markets that requires measurement, and that is the effect of these sales on sales in other, more developed markets. As noted previously, the process of developing better information and new products and processes for underserved markets sometimes provides insights that improve products and sales in mainstream markets. This can occur because of improved understanding of cultural, ethnic, and regional issues, or because of improvements in the product or distribution channel. Sales in underserved markets can also help to improve regulatory relations, as providing services to underserved communities can be an important goal for government agencies.

To capture this information efficiently, it is important to build on existing methods for tracking the impact of marketing and promotion activities. It is also important to develop ways to gather anecdotes and qualitative data from the sales force, which is most likely to see firsthand the impact on sales. Even though qualitative data may be considered "soft," an anecdote or example that clearly illustrates how the sales in underserved markets affected sales in mainstream markets can be extremely useful for management as it seeks to enhance this effect. For example, St. Paul Travelers' work in the Loss Prevention Partnership in underserved neighborhoods enabled its managers to understand and resolve a complex regulatory issue that affected its sales across an entire state, covering both mainstream and underserved markets. This helped managers to make the case for continued work in the Loss Prevention Partnership.

PUTTING IT ALL TOGETHER: CASE STUDY

By now, your head may be filled with possible strategies for improving your company's ability to compete in underserved markets. But how do they all fit together? What is the picture of an integrated strategy for reaching low-income consumers? Here is a case study of a company that has employed a full range of strategies to reach underserved markets profitably.

Fannie Mae

Fannie Mae is the leading source of capital for home mortgages in the United States. The company operates exclusively in the secondary market by purchasing mortgages and mortgage-related securities from loan originators such as banks and mortgage brokers. These purchases provide the capital required by originators to continue their lending activities.

Fannie Mae has successfully introduced new low-downpayment mortgages designed for low-income homebuyers in the United States. The company's decision to focus on serving this market was driven by two pressures: (1) regulatory pressure to provide better services to low-income individuals, and (2) recognition of the fact that most of the future growth in the mortgage market in the United States will come from low-income and immigrant households.

But figuring out how to serve the market for low-income individuals profitably was not easy. Financial products like mortgages and insurance are unusual in that the cost of the product is not known until long after the sale occurs. One of the key costs is loan loss—the loan principal that is not repaid. Most loan losses occur within three to eight years after the loan is made. In other words, bankers don't know the full cost of making a loan until three to eight years after they have made it.

To address this problem, banks and insurance companies collect and analyze enormous amounts of information in an attempt to determine which characteristics of the borrower and the home best predict repayment performance. At the point that Fannie Mae started to develop the low-downpayment mortgage in 1998, the best information available suggested that individuals who could only afford a small downpayment were a high risk. Similarly, individuals who did not have a credit record, or who had not been employed at the same job for three years or more, were likely to be a high risk. But these were precisely the characteristics of many of the low-income households that Fannie Mae wanted to serve, so the company needed to create a different kind of product.

For assistance in developing and testing a new product that could profitably serve these markets, Fannie Mae turned to Self-Help, a nonprofit community development lender that specializes in addressing the needs of those who are underserved by conventional lenders, particularly minorities, women, rural residents, and low-income families. Self-Help worked with Fannie Mae to develop better information about this market and to segment the market more finely to find pockets of profitable consumers that had previously been overlooked. For example, Self-Help identified the fact that low-income individuals who had the same income from year to year, even if employed at different jobs, were a good financial risk. This is because many low-income people in the United States often work at jobs with little job stability, and they have to be able to nimbly move from job to job as the market around them shifts. Self-Help also identified changes in Fannie Mae's business model that were required to lend profitably. In particular, Self-Help showed that pre-purchase counseling for first-time homebuyers, and a rapid intervention at the first sign of a late loan payment, helped to significantly reduce loan loss. As a result of their joint analysis, Fannie Mae was able to better understand the risks and costs of the market, and to define a new product for this market, incorporating a lower downpayment, changes in the definition of income in the underwriting standards, and new approaches to counseling and to responding to late payments.

Together with the Ford Foundation, Fannie Mae and Self-Help initiated a partnership in 1998 to bring this new product to scale. Through this partnership, Self-Help was able to (1) purchase affordable mortgages from banks that were making the mortgages, (2) bundle, and (3) credit-enhance them. The Ford Foundation provided funding that helped Self-Help to provide the credit enhancement. Fannie Mae then purchased the loans from Self-Help. The capital freed up through the sale of the mortgages was then loaned out again by the banks to create new affordable home mortgages. Initially, the product moved more slowly than expected. But then Fannie Mae changed the way it gave credit to its marketing staff for deals they helped to create between their customers and Self-Help. This helped to increase the attention that they paid to these deals, and the volume took off.

As of the end of 2003, Self-Help and Fannie Mae had achieved their goal of generating $2 billion in new affordable mortgages for low-income individuals. They also had been able to gather and analyze information on thousands of home loan payments, to better refine their business model. And over 30,000 previously underserved households could consider themselves homeowners at last.

Today, the market for low-downpayment mortgages has exploded. Fannie Mae, as the purchaser of these mortgages from banks, has developed a solid, high-volume, and profitable new line of business. In fact, this product has been so successful that Freddie Mac and GE Capital, Fannie Mae's primary competitors for purchasing mortgages, have created similar products (Ford Foundation, 2005; Fannie Mae, 2003).

Reading through this case study, we can see that Fannie Mae used four of the five strategies for success that this book emphasizes:

■ I. MINE AND TRANSLATE LOCAL MARKET INFORMATION

For Fannie Mae, being able to get better information on the specific behaviors of low-income consumers was critical to success. Through its pilot program in partnership with Self-Help and the Ford Foundation, Fannie Mae was able to gather and analyze information about loan performance that enabled it to pinpoint viable market segments within the low-income community and to understand the risk profile in detail.

■ 2. ADAPT BUSINESS MODEL TO COMMUNITY REALITIES

Fannie Mae had to revamp one of the most important elements of its business model—the criteria used to determine which borrowers were creditworthy. It also changed the features of the loans it purchased and required specific changes to loan servicing.

■ 3. CHANGE INTERNAL INCENTIVES AND CHALLENGE CULTURAL ASSUMPTION

Fannie Mae shifted the way it tracked and credited the deals that its marketing staff helped create, giving them more incentive to focus on the new product.

■ 4. CREATE PARTNERSHIPS AND STRATEGIC ALLIANCES

Fannie Mae was able to successfully leverage a partnership with Self-Help and the Ford Foundation to move into a new niche. The partnership enabled Self-Help and the Ford Foundation to achieve their goals as well, which were to change the market for home mortgages so that it now better serves the needs of low-income, previously underserved individuals.

■ CONCLUSION ■

Underserved communities offer significant potential for increased sales and revenue. Although most individuals in underserved communities have modest incomes, their aggregate purchasing power is enormous.

Increasing profitable sales in this market can pose challenges. The communities are often more heterogeneous than mainstream communities, which makes getting useful information about sales potential difficult. Companies may need to develop alternative sources of information, and adjust the way in which they analyze that information, to become knowledgeable about the communities and to decide where and how to market, to site stores, and to launch new products.

Unit costs can be higher in these communities, with distribution costs in particular often significantly higher. Residents may be distrustful of large companies, and some may feel strongly that the entry of large companies into their communities is a problem, not a benefit. The cautionary tale of Pathmark's entry into Harlem shows the level that these feelings can reach (see Introduction).

Creating a win-win relationship within underserved communities is one of the key strategies for addressing these challenges. Local businesses and nonprofits can serve as distribution channels, reducing costs and creating benefits for residents. Companies can help residents build income and assets by providing products at lower costs, hiring residents, and purchasing from local businesses. Two of the key arguments that Pathmark found persuasive to Harlem residents were that they would get higher-quality produce at lower prices and higher-paying jobs for residents. These factors were critical in addressing community resistance.

By creating a win-win relationship with underserved communities, your company can both improve profits and improve communities. You can help to build a world where everyone has access to high-quality goods at reasonable prices—and where residents of underserved communities benefit from this relationship as much as residents of mainstream communities do.

For additional case studies and further details, see the following websites:

Accountability: www.conversations-with-disbelievers.net
Win-Win Partners: www.winwinpartner.com
World Resources Institute: www.wri.org
World Business Council for Sustainable Development: www.wbcsd.org

2

RECRUITING AND RETAINING A QUALIFIED WORKFORCE

Do you worry about where your future workforce will come from? Have you tried to explore alternative sources for talent, but met with limited results? If these questions don't sound familiar, then skip this chapter—it's not for you. But if, like many managers, you see the need to expand the labor pools from which you can draw a qualified workforce, then dive into the details here.

When managers responsible for recruiting and retaining a qualified workforce first engage with underserved communities, they often encounter difficulties. They can have a hard time attracting qualified individuals. Recruits may not seem to understand the unwritten rules for how to get along in a workplace. Recruits may have problems with childcare and transportation that make their attendance erratic. They can have a very different set of priorities from the rest of the workforce. Even something as basic as speaking the same language can be a problem.

And yet, many companies have been very successful with a workforce drawn from underserved communities. This chapter shows you how they have adapted the five success factors to solve human resources (HR) challenges. We look at how to develop social networks that help you find the right employees, how to deploy cost-effective strategies to increase retention, and how partnerships with organizations in the community can help your employees advance in their careers.

UNDERSTANDING THE WORKFORCE CHALLENGE

Over the next two decades, the sources for new workers will change dramatically, both in the United States and abroad. In developed countries, the proportion of new workers coming from mainstream communities will shrink significantly. Most of the new workforce will come from underserved communities and from immigrants. In the developing world, exactly the opposite will happen. There will be a significant growth in the workforce, almost all of which will be driven by the dramatic increase in the proportion of young people in the population.

In the United States, where will tomorrow's workforce come from and what will be its characteristics? The fastest-growing labor pool includes minorities and immigrants. The U.S. Department of Labor predicts that between 2002 and 2012, the labor force growth rates of minority groups will substantially outpace that of whites in the United States: 33 percent for the Hispanic labor force, 19 percent for the black labor force, and 9 percent for the white labor force. According to Northeastern University's Center for Labor Market Studies, between 2000 and 2003, new immigrants contributed more than half of the growth in the nation's labor force, exceeding their contribution in the decade of the 1990s, which was a historical high in the United States. In 2003, there were 21.8 million immigrants employed, which accounted for nearly 15 percent of the U.S. labor force. Some segments of the immigrant population have a lower-than-average educational attainment, while others exceed national averages. For example, only 64 percent of new foreign immigrant workers have earned at least a high school diploma, which is lower than the percentage of the native-born labor force. But fully 28 percent of these new foreign immigrants have received a bachelor's degree or higher, which is slightly better than the percentage for U.S. native-born workers (Horrigan, 2004; Sum et al., 2004).

Not only will there be fewer workforce entrants from mainstream communities, but the skills requirements for new workers will increase, making recruitment even more difficult. For many employers, the skills of the entering workforce are a key to competitive performance. For example, Toyota recently chose Woodstock, Ontario, for its new 1,300-employee factory rather than areas in the southeastern United States. Many southern states were offering double the $125 million subsidy that Ontario provided to win the $800 million factory, yet Toyota declined the offer because its experience suggested that the low quality of skills in the entering workforce in the Southeast (including deficits in mathematics, reading, and work readiness skills) would end up costing the company more in the long run.

Toyota's experience is not unique. According to the national organization Jobs for the Future, having the proper fit when a person is hired yields a significant return on investment, reducing both turnover and the need for in-house training. The National Association of Manufacturers' Center for Workforce Success reports that increasing the level of worker education by one year boosts productivity by 8.5 percent in manufacturing. Further, a study by the National Bureau of Economic Research found that formal employer-provided training increases productivity anywhere from 10 to 16 percent (Caldwell, 2001). Training creates benefits for workers, too. It helps them to advance to better-paying jobs. It also tends to increase job satisfaction.

A variety of factors have made it increasingly difficult for employers both in the United States and elsewhere in developed countries to find workers that possess the skills needed in today's workplace. Key factors creating the skills gap in the United States are as follows:

- *Economic globalization.* Global pressures are squeezing U.S. business, particularly manufacturers, as they face brutal competition from around the world. To continue to succeed, U.S. manufacturers must compete less on cost than on product design, productivity, flexibility, quality, and responsiveness to customer needs. These competitive mandates put a high premium on the skills, morale, and commitment of workers.

- *Technology advances.* Relentless advances in technology have infused every aspect of business operations. Today's jobs are technology jobs, and employees at all levels must have the wide range of skills required to respond to the demands of an increasingly complex workplace environment, including mathematics, science, problem solving, communications, and teamwork.

- *Demographic shifts.* Experts predict that the convergence of several trends—declining births, retiring baby boomers, and expected business growth—will create more jobs than there will be workers to fill them by 2010. The Bureau of Labor Statistics (BLS) reports that the civilian labor force will increase by 17 million, reaching 158 million in 2010. But by then, the BLS expects the number of jobs will reach 168 million (Horrigan, 2004).

- *Educational shortfalls.* The American educational system is failing to provide the requisite preparation to perform well in today's workplace. "The harsh fact is that the U.S. need for the highest quality human capital in science, mathematics and engineering is not being met," says the U.S. Commission on National Security for the 21st Century. In a recent study, 15-year-olds in the United States ranked 24th out of 29 industrialized nations on practical math applications (American Association of Engineering Societies, 2002).

Old methods of recruiting, hiring, training, and advancing workers are not meeting the needs of either employers or employees. In a recent survey by the U.S. Chamber of Commerce, half of the employers polled indicated that they have a "hard" or "very hard" time finding qualified job applicants. A job-skills shortage is already occurring in the manufacturing industry and is likely to spread to other industries over the next 10 to 15 years as baby boomers retire. Shortages are expected in the global competition for managers, engineers, technicians, skilled craftspeople, and front-line workers, mostly jobs requiring a college degree or technical education. Experts say changes must occur on a broad front, from better technology and skills training in secondary schools to a coordinated national workforce policy (U.S. Chamber of Commerce, 2003).

This chapter shows you how to manage these complex and challenging trends. It explains how to create networks so that you can find the kind of recruits that you need. It discusses ways of engaging productive partners who can bring you skilled and experienced employees. It also shows you how to work with other businesses and nonprofit organizations to help fill the long-term pipeline of skilled workers by improving the quality of skills in the populations from which you recruit. By working together to put in place the training and supports required so that the new workforce entrants have the skills and abilities to succeed, business can ensure that it will have the appropriate workers when they are needed. This benefits communities as well as business, because it helps ensure residents have the skills they need to get steady employment and good wages.

UNLOCKING THE WORKPLACE OF THE FUTURE

■ I. MINE AND TRANSLATE LOCAL MARKET INFORMATION

What's Different about Underserved Markets?

If you are like most other HR managers, you know that you get many of your best recruits by word of mouth—people who work in your company now, or who worked there before, send along individuals they think would be a good fit. Why does this network perform well? Because the people doing the referring know you well, and they know the jobseekers well. They form a social network that helps jobseekers find out about your jobs and that pre-screens and connects jobseekers to jobs that are a good fit. The same individuals who send potential job candidates to you also may serve as references, providing accurate information about the jobseeker. In fact, HR experts estimate that 80 percent of all jobs, across all industries, are filled by word-of-mouth referrals. The best "local market information" for you and your job candidates comes from the social network that connects you (Forte Foundation, 2005)

As your business seeks to expand its hiring from underserved communities, you may find that your company doesn't connect effectively to the social networks in these communities, and they don't connect to your company. As a result, candidates have a hard time finding out about you, and you have a hard time finding out about them. The "local market information" that both of you need is missing. Companies have successfully

What's different?

- Social networks that enable businesses and jobseekers to find each other are weak or nonexistent.

What to do about it.

- Build connections to local institutions.
- Create new social networks and career pathways.

addressed this challenge by building connections to local institutions that are central nodes in the social networks of underserved communities, and by creating entirely new social networks and career pathways. Once you understand that the problem results from a lack of connection to potential recruits, you can work to create that connection in cost-effective ways.

What to Do in Underserved Markets

Build Connections to Local Institutions

Every community has many social networks threaded through it—connections between the individuals in the community that transmit information, requests, favors, and a sense of belonging. Businesses can identify institutions in the community where many of these networks come together in central nodes. These institutions are a natural place for people looking for work to seek information and access. Particular institutions vary from community to community, but they often include local churches, community-based nonprofits, community colleges, and city and state employment agencies. By creating mutually beneficial relationships with these organizations, businesses can (1) get accurate information out to potential jobseekers about the opportunities for work and advancement, and (2) gain access to a stream of job candidates who are pre-screened and appropriate for the jobs that the company is seeking to fill.

Manpower's TechReach program (see Introduction) has been successful in finding and placing skilled individuals from underserved communities into IT jobs. Part of its success was due to its nationwide partnership with the U.S. Department of Labor. This partnership created formal links and communication between Manpower's 1,150 offices across the United States and nearly all of the Department of Labor's 1,900 One Stop Career Centers. The One Stop Career Centers are an important resource for jobseekers in underserved markets across the United States. They provide services such as testing, counseling, résumé preparation, and information about careers, apprenticeships, and education. They provide information and referrals to employers. They are also the central connection point for public sector services—including unemployment benefits, food stamps, health plans, financial support, and services for the disabled—to unemployed or dislocated workers and their families.

Manpower created a formal process to share information between its offices and the local One Stop Career Centers. This process included site visits to Manpower from the One Stop staff, and vice versa, so that each had a better idea about the needs and resources of the other. It also included formal methods of communicating about job opportunities, skill requirements, candidate availability, pre-screening, and overall satisfaction with the stream of referrals. This process has led to a dramatic increase in the number of qualified candidates sent to Manpower by the One Stop Career Centers, and it has significantly increased the awareness in underserved communities about career opportunities that Manpower provides. By building connections to a network of local institutions—the One Stop Career Centers—Manpower was able to help establish a new social network that identified and referred appropriate candidates (Ford Foundation, 2005).

We need to add a cautionary note here, though. Even though creating linkages to local groups and institutions can be a valuable tool for recruiting candidates, it is critical to partner with community and job placement groups that truly understand your needs and are capable of working with them. Companies may find that the services

---

Management Tips: Choosing a Community Organization as a Partner

Choose a group that:

- understands your business and the prerequisite skills for the jobs you are trying to fill.
- takes the time to screen the individuals it is placing and develops a clear sense of their interests, abilities, and barriers to employment.
- is responsive and client-centered to employers—preferably, an organization that has one point of contact, is well organized and fully staffed, and has the ability to respond in a timely fashion.
- responds when it is notified that there are problems with the new employee who was just placed at your site.

Source: Winning Workplaces, 2005.

provided by these local groups and institutions vary dramatically in quality. Some provide excellent and well-customized service, while others attempt to fit every corporation and every jobseeker into a "one size fits all" mold. Particularly problematic are community groups that do not take the time to know the needs of employers' businesses or to understand the basic knowledge and skills required of entry-level candidates. In addition, some of the groups' screening processes are inadequate, and they do not provide enough job readiness training for the candidates.

To find a valuable community partner, consider the following questions in choosing a community organization to work with:

- How well does the group understand your business and the prerequisite skills for the jobs you are trying to fill?
- Does the organization take time to screen the individuals it is placing and to develop a clear sense of their interests, abilities, and barriers to employment?
- How responsive and client-centered is the organization in working with employers? For example, does it have one point of contact or several? Is its operation well organized and fully staffed? How capable is it of responding quickly to requests?
- How quickly and well does the organization respond when it is notified that there are problems with the new employee that was just placed at your site?

Using these questions as a guide, you will be able to identify the well-performing organizations and pick one as a partner that will help you to hire more quickly and more effectively (Winning Workplaces, 2005).

Create New Social Networks and Career Pathways

In some communities, there are no pre-existing networks that businesses can tap into to reach the right potential job candidates. There are also occasions where existing networks don't provide a pathway for individuals to move through educational channels to the kinds of careers that are available with particular employers.

The latter problem is particularly pressing for industries that have undergone major restructuring, such as advanced manufacturing in the United States. There is a dramatic disconnect between (1) the general perception in underserved communities about the job and career opportunities in this industry, and (2) the actual job opportunities today. For example, focus group and survey research conducted by the National Association of Manufacturers (NAM) shows that the predominant image of manufacturing among youth, their families, and counselors is that it is "dirty, dark, dangerous and declining." As a result, there is little demand for courses that could lead students in high school or community colleges to be ready for jobs in these industries, and there are few effective connections between employers and the educational system. Yet the reality, particularly for rapidly growing segments of advanced manufacturing such as biotech and semiconductors, is that there are jobs with high pay, good benefits, a career path, and a clean work environment (Eisen, 2005).

In order to address this challenge, manufacturers are making efforts to provide the potential future workforce with an understanding of why jobs in manufacturing are attractive, and what specific educational background is required to get and keep good jobs in this industry. For example, Advanced Micro Devices (AMD), one of the largest semiconductor companies in the United States, faced a shortage of skilled technicians in the mid-1990s. The dramatic growth of manufacturing jobs at its Austin, Texas, site produced intense competition among the semiconductor corporations for a local, skilled workforce. Expensive out-of-town recruitment costs and high turnover rates prompted AMD to act. The company took a leadership role in mobilizing a public-private partnership to develop and recruit skilled workers from an untapped pool—low-income and minority adults and youth. The effort became part of the company's survival strategy to maintain operations in the Austin area.

As a corporate partner in a consortium of companies, government agencies, and nonprofits, AMD helped design the Semiconductor Manufacturing Technician (SMT) degree program, an industry-wide vocational training program. The initiative focused on the predominately low-income Hispanic community in East Austin marked by high unemployment, under-resourced schools, and limited skill development and training for high-paying job opportunities. While an active participant in the SMT program, AMD was also heavily involved in local school-business partnerships. The company's desire to take its business-school partnerships to a higher, more strategic level resulted in the development of AMD's own school-to-work job training program—the Accelerated Careers in Education (ACE) program—which exposes high school students to careers in semiconductor manufacturing.

Working concurrently in developing both programs, AMD soon recognized that ACE could be a valuable pipeline for preparing high school graduates who were interested in entering the SMT program. Consequently, the company initiated a link between the two programs to expand the potential impact of the ACE program to the entire industry and school system. The ACE program grew to become a regional effort as other semiconductor companies became involved—a move that was essential to build the program's capacity and sustainability.

The ACE and SMT programs worked well through 2001, creating increased job opportunities for residents and helping AMD fill its need for a skilled workforce. By 2001, the high-tech economy was slowing down dramatically, and the need for new technicians dropped off. In fact, there were job losses in the region, and several high-tech plants closed. But AMD and its corporate partners in the semiconductor industry did not close the program. Rather, they shifted its focus from a short-term one that provided specific skills training to a longer-term one that improved science and math proficiency in high schools. They knew that the semiconductor industry traditionally was cyclical in its employment needs and were willing to invest during slow times to ensure an educated workforce for the next growth cycle. The partnership's history of success and a willingness to be flexible provided the resilience needed to turn a challenge into an opportunity, to expand the scope of its work, and to create long-term benefits for community and corporation alike.

■ 2. ADAPT BUSINESS MODEL TO COMMUNITY REALITIES

What's Different about Underserved Markets

If you are like most HR managers, you have policies and procedures that work well for your existing workforce. They are perceived as fair. They motivate. They help ensure that absenteeism is kept to a minimum and that grievances are dealt with quickly and appropriately. But if, like many HR managers, you apply the same policies and procedures to the workforce from underserved communities, you will likely find that they don't work as well. The underserved workforce has different needs and support requirements from those of the standard middle-class workforce. They often need different kinds of help with childcare, training, transportation, and flexible schedules. Applying existing HR approaches and services to the underserved workforce can lead to high turnover, low morale, and mediocre productivity. You have to adapt parts of your business model to work well with these individuals.

It can be helpful to consider three separate components of the HR process: workforce entry, retention, and advancement. Each has separate challenges. Companies that have succeeded in developing workforces from underserved communities have established strategies for each of these components.

What's different?

- New workforce has different culture, skills, support requirements, and interests from incumbent workforce. Existing HR approaches lead to high turnover, low morale, and mediocre productivity.

What to do about it.

Entry

- Provide training to employees and supervisors on "soft skills" needed to perform well in the workplace.
- Encourage mentoring relationships to enable successful integration.

Retention

- Help employees get access to supportive services.
- Develop HR systems tailored to new workforce needs.

Advancement

- Develop career ladders within and across firms.
- Build training opportunities tailored to new workforce needs.

What to Do in Underserved Markets

Workforce Entry

The entry period—the first 90 days on the job—is critical in shaping a new employee's future with the company. During this period, the employee has to come to understand and embrace the company culture—and the company has to determine whether there is a good fit between the employee and the job. This can be a difficult transition for any employee, which is why so many companies have a 90-day probationary period before conferring permanent status and benefits on their employees.

The entry period can be particularly critical when the company starts to draw in a workforce from a new and different culture and ethnicity, and when new hires from these communities are working for first-line supervisors that are drawn from a mainstream population. Cultural norms, some not even consciously articulated, often differ around such important issues as what constitutes timeliness and customer service, and what are appropriate reasons for being absent from the job. For example, in some cultures it is expected that a mother will stay home from work when her child is sick. In others, this would be seen as being uncommitted to the job. If such cultural differences are not understood and managed, both employers and employees are likely to be frustrated, and a high level of absenteeism and poor morale may result.

Training and orientation during the entry period constitute a critical contributor to success when hiring a workforce from an underserved community. This training and orientation often include not only the standard information about company policies and workplace procedures, but also the social skills and norms required to work well in the corporate culture such as how to interact with peers, resolve disagreements, and respond to customers. Some companies also provide training in communication and conflict resolution to supervisors as well as entry-level recruits.

The TJX Corporation's work in hiring individuals from under-

Management Tips: Strategies for Recruiting New Employees

- Develop relationships with school-to-career and college co-op programs.
- Use temporary agencies and staffing firms creatively.
- Support training to develop a supply of qualified candidates to fill job vacancies.
- Take advantage of the public workforce training system.
- Participate in pre-employment training programs.
- Hire significant numbers of immigrants who share a language.

Source: Jobs for the Future, 2003.

served communities who formerly had little or no work experience provides a good example. In the mid-1990s, TJX-owned retail stores such as Marshalls and TJMaxx were facing difficulties recruiting and retaining qualified entry-level people for their retail operations. The company saw the opportunity to increase its hiring from underserved communities at this time through the major push to move individuals from welfare to work. This provided not only a source of potential employees, but also some funding to help smooth the transition.

To address the potential difficulties in recruitment and retention, TJX created a partnership with Goodwill Industries, a nonprofit with a strong track record of training and placing physically challenged individuals into productive jobs. Goodwill developed First Step, a customized recruitment and training program for TJX. First Step included three weeks of classroom training, a three- to five-week "internship" in which students engaged in work with close supervision from Goodwill staff, and a year of on-the-job support from Goodwill job specialists. Goodwill also provided training for the supervisors for these new recruits, to help them understand and manage the cultural differences and expectations on both sides. First Step was funded in part with grants from U.S. federal agencies and in part from contributions from TJX.

The program helped to both attract and retain employees. The retention rate for new employees who went through this program was 20 to 30 percent higher than the average rate for hires from traditional sources of labor. The First Step program, which began in Boston with the partnership with Goodwill, has been replicated by TJX in Chicago, Philadelphia, Detroit, Atlanta, and Puerto Rico. While the nonprofit partners vary depending on the best fit in each market, the partnerships build on the knowledge gained through the TJX/Goodwill relationship. TJX plans to further expand the First Step program to other locations (Center for Corporate Citizenship, 2004). See the box on page 66 for tips from the experience of TJX and others on how to recruit employees from underserved communities.

Workforce Retention

What drives retention? HR research shows that key factors include the relationship of an employee with his or her boss, the opportuni-

---

Management Tips: Strategies for Retaining Your Employees

1. Provide information and training
   - Implement a mentoring program.
   - Develop communications skills of supervisors.
   - Provide diversity training.
   - Develop an internal orientation program with handbook.
   - Partner with organizations that provide coaching to workers.
2. Develop supportive services
   - Provide support for childcare.
   - Offer eldercare.
   - Provide assistance with transportation to work.
   - Offer an Employee Assistance Program.
3. Increase financial incentives
   - Provide information about government financial supports.
   - Provide flextime to help employees with special needs.
   - Tie wages to performance.
   - Offer financial counseling and other financial services.

Source: Jobs for the Future, 2003.

---

ties for advancement and increased pay, the job design, the quality of a company's products, and the perception that the company is a good corporate citizen. In addition, specific issues need to be addressed for a workforce coming from an underserved community, and these issues differ from community to community. It is important to assess the issues that matter for the community you are hiring from, and to develop a program for addressing them.

The Marriott Associates Hot Line is a good example of this type of assessment and program development. In 1993, Marriott examined the effectiveness of the company's work-life programs. It was concerned to find that these programs were not adequately meeting employee needs and that these unmet needs were adversely impacting job performance and customer service. Many employees were beset by complex, acute, and urgent life issues—car and transportation issues, language and immigration issues, abusive spouses, crime, drugs and alcohol, school problems of children, financial and legal problems, evictions and other housing issues, and on and on. Moreover, these problems did not come singly; employees tended to have two or more at a time. These problems resulted in high and poten-tially reducible rates of absenteeism, tardiness, and turnover among associates (Marriott's term for its employees). Moreover, managers and direct line supervisors reported that they were diverting up to 50 percent of their time to "social work" helping associates with such problems rather than spending it on their other managerial duties.

To address these issues, Marriott developed the Associate Resource Line, which provides confidential counseling through a one-stop resource that can address a wide range of personal issues. It is available via an 800 number to all covered Marriott managers and hourly employees, who may call an unlimited number of times from home or from a telephone set aside for this purpose on the Marriott property. The service is available 24/7 and is completely confiden-tial. All calls are handled by a staff of trained social workers.

Follow-up surveys indicated that 96 percent of the employees who used the service were satisfied with the help they received. As many as 63 percent reported reduced stress, 60 percent reported having more positive feelings about Marriott, and 23 percent reported lower absenteeism. Supervisors also reported that they were spending less time on "social work" and more time on managerial aspects of their jobs (Whiting, 1997).

Marriott piloted this program in Florida because of the large num-ber of Marriott properties there and the representative nature of that state's hourly Marriott workforce. A year later, the company expanded the test sites to Atlanta, Chicago, and Denver. As of 2005, the toll-free Associate Resource Line, is available in more than 100 languages to all Marriott associates (Bison.com, 2005). See the box on page 68 for tips from Marriott and others on how to retain employees from underserved communities.

Workforce Advancement

As noted previously, the opportunity for advancement and better pay is one of the keys to retention. In addition, many companies fill their midlevel and senior positions with people promoted from within. Advancement is a critically important strategy for workforce development as well as workforce retention and recruitment.

Portugal Telecom SA, the country's largest telecommunications com-

---

Management Tips: Strategies for Advancing Employees

1. Provide training
   - Cross-train employees.
   - Develop informal apprenticeships or on-the-job training programs.
   - Use local community colleges and other training providers.
   - Take advantage of slow periods to provide training.
   - Train employees in their native language.
2. Provide incentives.
   - Provide incentives for advancements.
   - Clearly outline advancement criteria.
   - Create Individual Development Plans for employees.
3. Work with industry peers
   - Develop training programs that meet industry needs.
   - Work with community colleges, chambers of commerce, and industry associations to develop comprehensive training programs.

Source: Jobs for the Future, 2003.

---

pany and a provider of international telecom services, provides an example of this approach. The company has developed the Qualificant Training Programme to help interested employees to increase their skills. The initiative is voluntary and is run after working hours. It involves 600 hours of professionally relevant training. Participants, who often lack educational qualifications for advancement in the company, work toward a certificate from the education ministry. As of 2004, the company had trained over 5,000 employees under the program.

The main aims of the Qualificant Training Programme are (1) to help less-skilled employees to succeed within the company, and (2) to increase staff mobility. The benefit to employees is that it enables them to move up the career ladder and enjoy increased responsibilities and pay. The benefit to the company is that it can now fill more mid-level positions with employees who are familiar with its operating structure and procedures. The program also increases employee loyalty and retention (CSR Europe, 2005). See the box above for tips on advancing employees from the experience of Portugal Telecom and others.

Companies may find, however, that the training and education required to enable employees to advance can be quite expensive—too expensive for companies to pay for by themselves. It also can be difficult and expensive for employees to get such training and education on their own without some type of assistance. As a result, there can be a critical bottleneck in the process of advancing employees to more senior positions in the firm.

To address this problem, companies often work together with training organizations and government agencies to create tailored training programs that meet both their needs and those of their employees. The companies provide guidance on the demand for trained workers and on the specific skills that the workers need to possess in order to advance. They may also help with curriculum development and training sites and equipment. In certain cases, they may even provide supervisors with release time in order to serve as teachers and trainers.

Genesis HealthCare's partnership with WorkSource Partners is a good example. Like many businesses in the long-term care industry, Genesis HealthCare, one of the United States' largest long-term and rehabilitation therapy providers, has been faced with acute workforce shortages. The Bureau of Labor Statistics projects that by 2010, direct care jobs (Registered Nurses, Certified Nurse Assistants, Home Health Aides) in the industry will grow to 2.7 million from 1.9 million in 2000—a 5.6 percent annual growth rate. Yet during the same period, BLS predicts only a 1.1 percent growth in the labor force. For Genesis HealthCare, the vacancy rate for Licensed Practical Nurses (LPNs) and Registered Nurses (RNs) is already 12.9 percent among its 45 New England region sites—equating to 161 vacancies. Compounding this supply problem are the anticipated retirements of 200 New England–based Genesis nurses in the next five years (from 2006 to 2010). In order to meet its staffing needs, Genesis New England Region is spending $3 million per year on staffing agencies (organizations that supply temporary nursing help for a fee).

Genesis HealthCare worked with WorkSource Partners, a training and workforce services provider, to develop the Campus on Campus program to help meet this growing need. Campus on Campus is a career advancement program that helps entry-level workers in Certified Nurse Assistant (CNA), housekeeping, and dietary positions move on tracks toward LPN and RN nursing jobs. The program follows a three-pronged approach: provide intensive case management to employees, facilitate access to education and training programs, and cultivate management support within the organization. It includes the provision of training and education services by local community colleges directly at the Genesis worksite. The program provides new career and job growth opportunities to current staff and offers a significant cost reduction to Genesis through increased retention rates and a reduced need for temporary agency hires.

Campus on Campus began operation in Agawam, Massachusetts, in the spring of 2001. The model is currently in place in three locations, two with Genesis facilities and one with an alliance of 11 long-term care facilities. Since 2001, as a result of the services available at these locations, over 700 employees have received career counseling and case management support, and nearly 50 new LPNs have graduated. CNA retention and turnover costs were reduced by over 75 percent from 2002 to 2004. Open positions dropped from 17 full-time and 17 part-time to 3 full-time and 11 part-time. Most impressive, agency fees dropped from $500,000 every six months down to zero.

The Campus on Campus program is now being expanded across the Genesis system sites in Massachusetts and in parts of Connecticut (Jobs for the Future, 2005).

■ 3. CHANGE INTERNAL INCENTIVES AND CHALLENGE CULTURAL ASSUMPTIONS

What's Different about Underserved Markets

Bringing in a workforce from underserved communities can pose challenges to your organization's culture and core assumptions. The new workforce may look different, talk in different ways, and have different body language and norms about nonverbal communication. The increase in diversity across the workforce must be managed well if the company and the employees are to benefit. While managing diversity well is a value in itself, it also can have positive consequences for your bottom line. Indeed, failure to manage diversity can have serious consequences: increased employee absence and turnover, reduced efficiency of communication, and increased conflict in work teams (Cox and Beale, 1997).

The key question, then, is how to change your company's internal culture so that it welcomes, retains, and advances a workforce that is very different from your current one. Companies use a variety of approaches. They create programs and use techniques that help employees to become more aware of the issues created by cultural diversity. They develop goals and measure performance on advancement and retention of employees from underserved communities. They also provide a "safe space" in which to raise concerns and resolve conflicts.

What's different?

- Dramatic increase in workforce diversity, if not managed well, can lead to miscommunication, misunderstanding, and conflict.

What to do about it.

- Increase awareness of issues created by cultural diversity.
- Develop goals and measure performance on advancement and retention.
- Create "safe space" to raise concerns and resolve conflicts.

What to Do in Underserved Markets

Increase Awareness of Issues Created by Cultural Diversity

If diversity is to be managed well, it must be understood. The first step is to raise awareness throughout the company that diversity exists in many forms, and that everyone in the company needs to be aware of the many faces of diversity and to understand their own role in addressing the issues that diversity creates in the company. This varies significantly from company to company and country to country. A second step involves acknowledging how the failure to address diversity can create problems for the company. While treating everyone with equal respect and dignity is a right in itself, it can be helpful to link improved performance in managing diversity to key drivers of success for the company.

Many companies use some type of diversity training as a way of raising awareness and promoting behavioral change. If you decide to use such training, it is important to be clear up front about what the goals are and how you will measure success. Is the training about awareness? behavior change? teamwork? communication? Because different groups within the organization are likely to see training from different perspectives, being as clear as possible about the goals can head off misunderstandings and conflicts.

The training is also likely to be unpopular with some employees, who may challenge the need for it or the authority of the trainers. It's a good idea to use trainers who have considerable experience with companies that are similar to yours; this helps validate their positions in explaining how improvements in managing diversity can help all employees get their jobs done better with less miscommunication and conflict.

Develop Goals and Measure Performance on Advancement and Retention of Employees

"What gets measured gets managed" is all too often true. In order to make progress at improving the way a company manages diversity, it is critical to have measurable goals and to track progress against those goals. This was one element of the dramatic turnaround at Texaco in the late 1990s. Texaco had initially done a poor job of managing diversity—such a poor job, in fact, that it was successfully sued for discrimination. In 1996, it paid $176 million to settle a class-action suit brought on behalf of approximately 1,400 current and former African American employees (Alexander, 2000). This suit led to a dramatic change of heart at Texaco, which subsequently committed itself to becoming a leader in diversity in the United States. As of 2002, minorities accounted for nearly four in ten of new hires and more than 20 percent of the promotions at Texaco. In fact, women and minorities together accounted for 67 percent of the new hires and 66 percent of the promotions at Texaco in 2002 (Ford Foundation, 2005).

What was Texaco's secret? It started at the top and instituted changes in awareness, communications, and procedures regarding diversity that cascaded down through the organization. Equally important, it set specific company-wide goals for hiring, retention, and advancement. These were broken down by division, and managers were held accountable for achieving specific targets in their area. Managers have to understand that diversity is important and that managing it is part of their job (Weiser and Zadek, 2000).

Create a "Safe Space" to Raise Concerns and Resolve Conflicts

Part of the challenge of integrating a diverse workforce is that it challenges assumptions and cultural norms that are often tacit. Managers, front line supervisors, and coworkers for the new workforce need to understand their own norms and assumptions, and how these interact with those of members of the new workforce. This can be difficult, deeply personal work, which is often hard to do under the stress and pace of daily workplace demands. It also can be sensitive and conflict-laden. Individuals sometimes are unaware of how their actions may be perceived across cultural boundaries, and getting feedback can be difficult.

Successful companies create processes and spaces where it is safe to raise these issues and where people have the time to hear and absorb feedback, and to explore their attitudes. This can happen, for example, at a diversity workshop or diversity training. Some companies integrate diversity issues into their 360 degree feedback processes, in which individuals get feedback on their performance from their peers and subordinates as well as from their supervisor. For this type of feedback to be useful for learning, it must be separated from compensation decisions; otherwise, it will be difficult for individuals to hear and accept negative feedback because it threatens their pay. This doesn't foster a welcoming environment for personal growth and change.

Another, more extensive approach involves what might be termed "learning journeys," in which individuals or groups from the company go on field trips ranging from one day to several weeks. For example, Business in the Community in the United Kingdom has led over 3,000 executives on trips into underserved communities to understand firsthand the culture, norms, and rhythms of life and work in these communities, and how residents can be better integrated into mainstream business as customers and employees (International Business Leaders Forum, 2005).

Companies also use techniques such as an ombudsman or a "hot line" to create a space for individuals to raise and discuss concerns. This approach is particularly important for addressing issues with supervisors or managers. The most important factor in determining retention is the relationship between supervisor and employee. Integrating the new workforce depends critically on the quality of this relationship. But raising concerns with one's boss about how he or she is handling diversity can be extremely difficult. Having an ombudsman provides an opportunity for employees to discuss their concerns and for the company to take action if needed.

■ 4. CREATE PARTNERSHIPS AND STRATEGIC ALLIANCES

What's Different about Underserved Markets

If you or your industry needs to build a pipeline of talent from underserved communities to meet business needs over the next several years, you may face problems. The individuals who could become attractive candidates may not know about your firm or industry, or they may not understand the opportunities that a career in your firm or industry could offer them. In the United States, these problems are particularly pressing for industries that require a strong science or math background, such as engineering and accounting. Individuals who have the aptitudes and abilities that would enable them to be very attractive candidates are not aware of the career opportunities and so don't take the kinds of courses or jobs that could put them on a track to a career in these industries. As a result, firms have a very hard time recruiting qualified candidates from underserved communities in the United States.

In addition to lacking knowledge about the industry, individuals may lack the academic and technical skills needed to succeed in today's business settings. This section will focus just on industry-specific technical skills training, not on fundamental academic preparation. Addressing the failure of an educational system to adequately prepare students with the requisite academic skills calls for a deeper and more profound systemic intervention, which we describe in the next section (see page 81).

What's different?

- Costs of attracting, training, and retaining workforce are too expensive for an individual company to bear alone.

What to do about it.

- Create local/regional partnerships for training and workforce development.
- Develop industry-wide coalitions to fund attraction and recruitment.

What to Do in Underserved Markets

Your company may decide to work by itself in taking on the full cost of attracting qualified candidates and helping those with the right background to get the training they need. Companies often do this for specific job categories in which there is a limited number of jobs to fill, and which are critical to their organizations' success. But when the numbers of individuals to be reached start to grow, and the kind of training required expands, taking on the whole cost often becomes too much to bear alone. In these cases, even the biggest and most profitable companies create partnerships with nonprofits and government agencies in order to fund the attraction, training, and skills certification of workers from underserved communities.

It can help to differentiate partnerships into two types:

- local/regional partnerships for industry-specific training and workforce development
- industry-wide coalitions that (1) fund communications campaigns to attract appropriate candidates, and (2) develop skills certification processes that enable workers to move more easily from school to work or from job to job.

Establish Partnerships for Training and Development

Partnerships for industry-specific training and development typically focus on a city, region, labor market area, or set of states. They help companies meet a specific set of labor market needs in that geographic area by working with the economic development, training, and educational organizations in the area to identify places where there is a demand for a particular type of employee or set of job skills that isn't being met, or cannot be met, by the existing institutions. They play a linking role between employer and employee. The partnerships help to track and communicate the job demands for their industry, and they monitor the pipeline of available talent. They help to guide and fund what is taught at the educational institutions, including community colleges, community-based organizations, and high schools. They help to organize visits to their workplaces, and they sponsor internships and externships. Finally, they connect potential employees with opportunities for training and education, and with jobs in the region. The semiconductor technician training that AMD helped to create is a good example (see page 63).

Develop Industry-wide Approaches to Fund Attraction and Recruitment

In addition to regional approaches, some businesses develop industry-wide strategies to fund the attraction and recruitment of individuals in the new workforce. This typically occurs when the industry as a whole is having difficulty recruiting talent from readily available pools of potential candidates. The industry leadership recognizes the need to act together, because all of them will benefit if they can improve the attractiveness of the industry to the potential labor force. The costs of attracting a workforce across the nation can be quite high, and the entire industry benefits from the effort, so the most appropriate vehicle for funding and directing the effort is usually an industry association.

National campaigns to attract a new workforce usually focus on creating awareness and removing barriers. The goals of such campaigns are to let the potential workforce know that jobs are going unfilled, where those jobs are, and why those jobs are attractive; and to inform potential employees about what kinds of skills, experience, and education are required to successfully get the jobs. Such campaigns may have to counter negative perceptions about the jobs—that they are unsafe, or boring, or dead-end. They may also have to address legal or regulatory barriers.

The National Association of Manufacturers (NAM) is a good example of an industry association that has taken on the task of creating awareness and interest among members of a new workforce. Being the largest industrial trade association in the United States, representing small and large manufacturers in every industrial sector and in all 50 states, NAM is well positioned to take on a critical problem facing U.S. manufacturers over the next decade: a growing difficulty in attracting employees with the right mix of skills to meet the needs of modern manufacturing settings.

This skills shortage is driven by two fundamental issues. The first is the demographic shift under way in the manufacturing workforce: current employees in the baby-boom generation will retire in ever larger numbers, beginning now and peaking in 2010, and take their experience and skills out of the workforce. These individuals will be replaced by a workforce that looks much different, with higher percentages of immigrants, minorities, and women. Attracting skilled candidates from this labor pool to jobs in manufacturing, and integrating them well when they arrive, constitutes a significant challenge.

The second issue is the widespread negative perception of jobs in manufacturing. NAM's research shows that the workforce of the future and those that shape its opinions—youth, their parents, their teachers, and the general public—often see manufacturing as offering primarily dark, dirty, dangerous, dead-end assembly-line jobs. This contrasts sharply with the fact that manufacturing jobs in the United States are typically well paid—in 2004, the average manufacturing compensation was $63,000 per year, and 84 percent of manufacturing workers received direct health benefits. Most assembly-line jobs have left the United States, and those that remain generally involve working with computer-controlled equipment in well-lit, air-conditioned settings. NAM's research also confirmed that in most public schools, teachers and counselors have and provide little or no information on career options in modern manufacturing.

To address this situation, in 2005 NAM launched the "Dream It. Do It." campaign, a national effort with the goal of "making manufacturing a preferred career option by the end of this decade." The campaign integrates national and local efforts to change perception and attract the new workforce through three interlocking strategies:

1. *Improve perceptions of jobs in manufacturing.* NAM is mounting an awareness campaign targeted at 18- to 26-year-olds (and their parents and teachers) who are making career choices. The campaign uses a range of communications approaches, including Web-site and radio and print advertising, to correct perceptions and stereotypes about manufacturing and to stimulate interest in manufacturing career options.

2. *Provide career information, guidance, and linkages to training and jobs.* Using both national and local resources, the campaign is designing and implementing an array of events, information, and partnerships to connect those interested in jobs with advice, education, training, and career opportunities. These efforts reach

into the schools and postsecondary institutions, as well as to young adults who are out of school.

3. *Address gaps in local education and training for manufacturing.* On the local level, the pipeline of education and training in preparation for manufacturing is being identified and assessed for quality and for relevance to manufacturing's evolving needs. Gaps are being identified, and teams of educators and employers are working to align education and training programs with employer and workforce needs.

Because the campaign is still in its initial stages, one cannot assess its overall impact. But the preliminary results have been encouraging, with a high level of interest shown by target audiences (18–26-year-olds) in Kansas City and other locations where the campaign has kicked off. Potentially even more important, the campaign suggests that a national organization can play a key role in helping to attract and recruit a workforce from a new labor pool (National Association of Manufacturers, 2005).

■ 5. IMPROVE THE ENABLING ENVIRONMENT

What's Different about Underserved Markets

The enabling environment includes laws, regulations, infrastructure, and institutions that support and shape the context in which business works. Critical elements of the enabling environment shaping the workforce context are educational institutions, transportation, housing, and social services. Businesses cannot attract, retain, and advance a workforce that doesn't have adequate education and skills training, that can't get to work, or that doesn't have the social services (childcare, healthcare, housing, etc.) required to be focused, attentive, and fully present at work.

What to Do in Underserved Markets

Education and Training

The education and training of the current and future workforce is one of the key drivers of business success. It is also a task that far exceeds what most businesses can tackle by themselves. Helping to improve the entire educational pipeline, from primary through post-secondary education, is a task that usually requires a business coalition or industry association. Individual businesses can and often do partner with specific schools in very produc-tive ways. But helping to shape the whole system so that it better meets the skills-training needs of both employers and employees requires a group effort. Similarly, working to improve transportation, childcare, or other social services requires businesses to speak with a united voice. In most cases, such tasks must be addressed community by community, because control of the educational and social services systems rests with the city, region, or state.

> **What's different?**
>
> ▪ Workforce is not being ade-quately prepared by educational institutions and is not sup-ported by social services.
>
> **What to do about it.**
>
> ▪ Build coalitions to improve education and social services infrastructure.
> ▪ Work to change governance of workforce development sys-tem.

In many communities in the United States, the education and training system does not adequately prepare the future workforce for jobs in local businesses, which makes it difficult for local businesses to attract and retain a skilled workforce. This is particularly true for posi-tions that do not require a college degree. Recognizing this, three national organizations—the U.S. Chamber of Commerce Center for Workforce Preparation, the National Association of Manufacturers Center for Workforce Success, and Jobs for the Future—collaborated to create the Workforce Innovation Networks (WINs) project. This project focused on helping local employer organizations—chambers of commerce, business and industry associations, and the like—to act effectively to create improvements in educational institutions and workforce training organizations. The goal was twofold:

1. to enable employers to better meet their need to recruit, develop, and advance productive entry-level workers;
2. to improve the ability of the non-college-bound population to obtain "family supporting" jobs and career paths.

Management Tips: Help to Build Your Future Workforce

- Provide leadership in efforts to raise the quality of the nation's education and skills pipeline.
- Engage in partnerships—with schools, school systems, networks of schools, and states—that advocate for, support, and enable the startup and long-term success of high-quality schools.
- Work with high schools and postsecondary institutions to define the critical skills and knowledge that students need to succeed in the workplace.
- Provide hands-on learning experiences, such as internships, that give students real-world work experience and expose them to career options.
- Collaborate with postsecondary institutions and workforce development systems to create explicit career paths that link ongoing education to career advancement in the firm or industry.
- Become learning-friendly workplaces by providing upfront tuition payment for entry-level workers, career and educational counseling, and flexible work schedules.

Source: Jobs for the Future, 2005.

The WINs project helped build the capacity of local employer organizations through training and technical assistance, development and dissemination of "best practices" materials, creation of peer learning networks, and assistance in raising funds to undertake special projects. The local employer organizations undertook a range of tasks to better align the activities of the workforce development system with the needs of employers and employees alike, including the following:

- Convene and support employers
- Broker and provide services
- Improve education, training, and supportive services
- Conduct research and development
- Help govern/improve the workforce development system. (Jobs for the Future, 2004)

The WINs project worked in depth with 25 cities, regions, and states. Many of the employer organizations were able to make a significant impact on their local workforce systems. For example, the Manufacturers' Association of South Central Pennsylvania partnered with the local Workforce Investment Boards in several regions to develop funding, contact companies, identify training needs, and coordinate training. As a result, the association obtained grants to train 850 workers in more than 40 companies, large and small, including Harley Davidson and Starbucks. In Oklahoma, Tulsa WINS! provided direct support to the economic development activities of the Tulsa Metro Chamber of Commerce to meet the hiring, training, and outplacement needs of employers. This resulted in hiring, screening, and referrals for over 1,500 new jobs in the region. For instance, IC of Oklahoma hired 100 employees. Other customers included First Data Corporation; Vanguard Car Rental USA, Inc.; EchoStar; DirecTV; and State Farm. Several employer associations participated, including the Tulsa Aerospace Alliance and the Oklahoma Alliance for Manufacturing Excellence (U.S. Chamber of Commerce, 2002; Jobs for the Future, 2005). See the box on page 82 for more tips from the WINs Project and others on how to help build a future workforce.

Supportive Services

Business can play a critical role in influencing policy, legislation, and regulation in ways that promote the social service supports—childcare, healthcare, housing, etc.—that individuals from underserved communities require. Helping to shape policy so that it better meets the needs of underserved communities is both a matter of social justice and good business. Better meeting these needs enables individuals from underserved communities to be productive, healthy, long-term employees.

Corporate Voices for Working Families is a good example of how business coalitions can shape policy, legislation, and regulation. Corporate Voices for Working Families is a U.S.-based nonpartisan, nonprofit corporate membership organization that brings the private-sector voice into the public dialogue on issues affecting working families. Collectively, its 52 partner companies employ more than 4 million individuals throughout all 50 states, with annual net revenues of $800 billion.

Corporate Voices and its partner companies work with Congress and the White House on issues related to working families that are not typically addressed through corporate government relations offices. Corporate Voices advances public policy development that better supports working families by:

- articulating the bipartisan "bottom line" for businesses of working family policies and practices
- communicating the value of public policy investments in working family policies
- bridging public, private, and nonprofit sectors on working family policies
- creating a forum for learning, partnership, and networking
- demonstrating a commitment to corporate citizenship
- tracking current emerging policy trends and their impact.

One example of how Corporate Voices shapes the enabling environment to provide better supports for individuals from underserved communities is its work on business and public policies that assist low-wage workers. In April 2004, Corporate Voices released *Increasing the Visibility of the Invisible Workforce: Model Programs and Policies for Hourly and Lower Wage Employees*. This report provided evidence showing how the provision of benefits to low-wage earners improves the corporate bottom line. The benefits studied included dependent care, employee development, financial assistance, and flexible scheduling. A study of 15 model programs reported positive impacts on employee attraction, retention, and increased worker productivity. These programs also help employees to better meet family needs, save for the future, and balance the demands of work and family. Corporate Voices' members also testified on similar issues affecting working families before a hearing of the Children & Family Subcommittee of the U.S. Senate Health, Education, Labor & Pensions (HELP) Committee. By bringing attention to the importance of these issues for low-wage workers, and to the business benefits that these supports can create, Corporate Voices helped to open up new and creative approaches in the development of business and public policy including new ways of organizing, delivering, and funding these programs (Corporate Voices for Working Families, 2005).

Transportation and Housing

Many business coalitions seek to improve housing and transportation in their regions. For example, Chicago Metropolis 2020 is working to promote affordable housing in the Chicago area. Chicago Metropolis 2020 is a business-led advocacy organization whose mission is to foster collaborative action to strengthen the economic vitality and quality of life in the six-county Chicago region. In 2001, Chicago Metropolis 2020 conducted a quantitative study that concluded that the lack of affordable housing near job sites (1) was costing businesses $200 to $250 million per year, and (2) was leading to inequities and a lower quality of life for employees. This finding helped support a 40-point Workforce Housing Action Agenda issued by Metropolis in 2002. The Action Agenda called for local zoning reforms and increased emphasis on building code enforcement and property maintenance by local governments; increased state government assistance and rewards to communities that create a broad range of housing; expansion and improvement of federal programs to increase affordable housing; and corporate action to create workforce housing.

In Chicago, housing issues have traditionally been pushed by non-profit advocates, but once the business community became involved, the issue drew more attention. Metropolis is now regarded as a key player on the housing issue and has worked hard to get affordable housing on the state agenda. Along with the Metropolitan Planning Council and Business and Professionals for the Public Interest, Metropolis successfully asked the legislature and governor in 2003 to create an affordable housing task force. The task force is charged with developing a statewide affordable housing plan, and it is highly likely that some or all of their recommendations will be adopted in the coming legislative session. And, after intensive lobbying by Metropolis 2020, the State of Illinois began an affordable-housing tax credit that matches the employers' contributions to affordable housing dollar for dollar. This benefits low-income individuals by increasing the amount of affordable housing. It also benefits businesses because it enables workers to live much closer to the suburban locations where many businesses operate, making it easier for them to attract and retain a stable workforce (Ford Foundation, 2005).

MEASURING PROGRESS

What measures can help you track and manage recruiting, retention, and advancement of individuals from underserved communities? Human resource professionals have developed a wide range of measures that address employee productivity, absenteeism and lateness, turnover rate, promotion rate, and recruitment yield. What are the unique issues that require special attention and measurement when hiring from underserved communities?

First and foremost, managers need data on how well the company is integrating the new workforce into the operations. They need data on hiring, performance, promotion, and retention—broken down in ways that demonstrate how the workforce is faring. For example, a manager might want to know the percentage of applicants from different groups that are hired, and what the 90-day retention rate is by group. This would illustrate how well the company is doing at attracting the right kinds of candidates and screening them appropriately.

It is important to include perspectives from diverse groups in designing the success metrics, questionnaires, and methods of gathering the information. It is also important to seek expert counsel to ensure that you don't violate any laws or create the appearance of singling out one group for preferential treatment.

Second, managers need to understand where conflicts are occurring, and what steps to take to resolve them. Many companies develop ways to sense and address conflict by creating ombudsmen and help lines. It is important to provide ways for conflicts to come to the surface safely without destroying the working relationship in a unit. It is equally important to address the underlying causes of the conflict, particularly when they arise from different perceptions about what kinds of behavior are acceptable. Another tool, exit interviews, can shed light on concerns and conflicts that employees might not be willing to voice before they decide to leave the firm.

Finally, it can be helpful to track the ways in which a diverse workforce spurs innovation, customer insight, and team creativity. We address this concept more fully in Chapter 4. In capturing these insights, qualitative measures are valuable: stories from operations, sales, and R&D illustrating how having a diverse team is helping to achieve their goals. It also may be useful to circulate stories and examples of best practices in this regard.

PUTTING IT ALL TOGETHER: CASE STUDY

DreamWorks SKG and Workplace Hollywood provide a good example of how an industry and a nonprofit can work together to hire talented employees from underserved communities.

DreamWorks SKG is a leading producer of live action motion pictures; animated feature films; network, syndicated, and cable television programming; home video and DVD entertainment; and consumer products. Workplace Hollywood is an industry-sponsored nonprofit whose mission is to train and prepare people from historically underrepresented and economically disadvantaged communities in Los Angeles to effectively compete for, and gain access to, jobs and business opportunities in the entertainment industry.

The impetus for the creation of Workplace Hollywood came from Jeffrey Katzenberg, one of the three founding partners of DreamWorks SKG, who was deeply concerned that individuals from minority and economically disadvantaged communities were not finding their way into jobs in the entertainment industry. Katzenberg recognized that this was due in significant part to the fact that jobs in the industry tended to follow personal relationships, and that these relationships typically did not reach deeply into minority and economically disadvantaged communities. He spearheaded the drive to create diversity at DreamWorks SKG and eventually led the effort to create Workplace Hollywood. He and his partners, Steven Spielberg and David Geffen, each contributed $1 million personally to start the nonprofit.

Workplace Hollywood's board includes senior executives from all the major studios, public sector leaders, and executive directors from community-based organizations. The board provides guidance on the structure and content of the training Workplace Hollywood provides, and it helps to connect Workplace Hollywood into both the underserved community and the media industry. The senior executives on the board also typically have the mandate within their own organizations to increase diversity and to integrate the new workforce into their operations.

Workplace Hollywood acquaints high school students with the wide variety of careers in media by offering an array of internship opportunities, both paid and for school credit. Internships are provided in film and television, animation, music, business affairs, finance, information technology, and other disciplines. Workplace Hollywood helps prepare students and young adults for work by offering training and education, both directly and through partnering training organizations. Workplace Hollywood is currently targeting positions such as office assistants, production assistants, and entry-level union positions. By working with human resource departments and production professionals—including production coordinators, unit production managers, producers, and union business representatives—Workplace Hollywood is able to get the best and most up-to-date information on what should be taught in the classes and what jobs are in most demand.

Workplace Hollywood has received strong support from the Hollywood unions, leading to the creation of the Workplace Hollywood Union Apprenticeship Program. This program offers training for entry-level positions in a growing number of crafts. The unions fully support this effort and have established a new category in the basic union agreement to include a teacher/mentor. The unions participating in the program as of 2004 include: Local 44, affiliated property craftspersons; Local 80, grips; Local 729, set/sign painters; Local 816, scenic/graphic artists; Local 600, cinematographers; Local 705, costumers; Local 706, make-up artists and hair stylists; and Local 700, editors.

Workplace Hollywood has grown to significant scale in a short period. As of the end of 2004, it had a database of 4,000 screened job candidates (a significant portion of the total entertainment industry employment of 45,000 in Los Angeles). Workplace Hollywood and its partnering training organizations had trained approximately 3,100 individuals and made 1,110 placements as of the end of 2004.

Workplace Hollywood illustrates all five key elements for success in building win-win relationships with underserved communities:

■ 1. MINE AND TRANSLATE LOCAL MARKET INFORMATION

One of the insights that led to the creation of Workplace Hollywood was the understanding that people get jobs in Hollywood based in part on their social networks. When looking for craftspeople to work on a film, producers tend to start with people they know or people recommended to them by individuals they trust. Thus, Workplace Hollywood needed to develop new social networks in order to enable individuals from underserved communities to get jobs in the industry. Workplace Hollywood did this in a number of ways. It serves as a broker, a trusted source for recommendations between community and industry. It also creates opportunities for people from the community and the industry to meet and develop relationships through internships and training opportunities. The fact that Workplace Hollywood was able to convince the unions to allow their members to work as teachers in its programs was significant; it meant that the classroom could become a place for creating connections between industry and community.

■ 2. ADAPT BUSINESS MODEL TO COMMUNITY REALITIES

Workplace Hollywood recognizes that individuals in the underserved community come from a different cultural context and so might not understand or succeed in the industry culture without training and support. In addition to training on technical skills, Workplace Hollywood helps individuals learn the critical "soft skills"—unstated expectations across the industry and how to meet them. Classes such as "Production Assistant Boot Camp" help individuals from the community get ready for the realities of work in Hollywood.

Workplace Hollywood also encourages mentoring relationships to enable successful integration into the workday world. It helps individuals from the community connect up with union and craft members in the industry through classes and mentorships to enable them to develop long-term relationships.

■ 3. CHANGE INTERNAL INCENTIVES AND CHALLENGE CULTURAL ASSUMPTIONS

Executives from the entertainment industry that sit on the Workplace Hollywood board typically are those who have the tasks of (1) increasing the awareness of issues created by cultural diversity in their own organizations, and (2) addressing the tensions and concerns that these issues can raise. By working to involve their frontline staff and supervisors in the Workplace Hollywood programs, these executives give their employees firsthand understanding of the new workforce and improve their ability to work with these individuals when they are hired.

■ 4. CREATE PARTNERSHIPS AND STRATEGIC ALLIANCES

By setting up Workplace Hollywood, the film and entertainment companies created a cost-effective way for all of them to build mutually beneficial partnerships with local institutions and communities. The task of establishing relationships with community colleges, community-based organizations, and government agencies is streamlined and more efficient by having one central organization—Workplace Hollywood—serve as a broker that connects all the organizations. The win-win nature of the relationship is evident in the ability of Workplace Hollywood to help community members find good jobs and to help industry members cultivate a skilled entry-level workforce.

■ 5. IMPROVE THE ENABLING ENVIRONMENT

Because Workplace Hollywood is in part an industry coalition that speaks with one voice about its needs and requirements, it has an impact on shaping the educational and training system that is far beyond what any one company could accomplish. Workplace Hollywood collaborates with a wide range of educational institutions to change the educational curricula and training offerings. It helps tailor them to the day-to-day needs of the entertainment industry, so that the individuals who graduate from the programs have skills to succeed in the industry. It provides accurate information on the future workforce needs of the entertainment industry to counselors and educators, so that they can help individuals make better choices about what kinds of jobs to pursue and the training that is required. Finally, Workplace Hollywood enables skilled craft union members to serve as teachers and trainers, which improves the ability of educational institutions to provide training that meets industry needs.

■ CONCLUSION ■

Workforce growth in the United States and Europe over the coming decades will come primarily from underserved communities. Although many individuals from these communities are talented, motivated, and well educated, companies can face significant hiring challenges.

The social networks that connect job seekers in these communities to employers in mainstream communities are often limited. Because most jobs are filled by word of mouth, it is often difficult for job candidates to find the right employer, and vice versa. When employees from underserved communities are hired by companies with primarily mainstream workforces, there can be difficulties in managing cultural differences, especially differences that stem from unstated assumptions about communication, conflict, and respect.

To address these challenges, companies tap into existing social networks by partnering with local community institutions or work to create new social networks. They develop specific strategies and programs for understanding and managing cultural differences and for helping all members of their workforce to build cultural competencies. Companies also create training programs, advancement opportunities, and benefits packages that better address the needs and interests of the new workforce.

Shortcomings in the enabling environment also pose challenges for hiring and retaining employees. In many undeserved communities, the system for educating the future workforce and providing them with technical traing needs to be significantly improved so that all graduates have the skills needed to succeed in today's competitive workforce. Transportation systems, child care, and housing also may be inadequate, making it difficult for potential employees to get to work and stay at work.

Many companies have taken on these challenges and work in partnership with other businesses and community organizations to improve local school systems and workforce training systems. They advocate for improvements in transportation, housing, and child care so that all residents of these communities can take advantage of jobs in their companies—not just those who are lucky enough to live on the right bus line or near affordable child care.

By taking on these challenges, your company can help build a pipeline of talent to meet your needs for a motivated, well-educated workforce and also to create opportunities for residents of under-served communities who need family-supporting jobs and meaning-ful careers.

For additional case studies and further details, see the following websites:

Center for Workforce Success: www.dreamit-doit.com
Initiative for a Competitive Inner City: www.workforceadvantage.org
Jobs for the Future: www.jff.org
Win-Win Partners: www.winwinpartner.com

3

INCREASING VALUE IN THE SUPPLY CHAIN

If you were to randomly pick any company's seasoned purchasing manager and tell him or her that there were great opportunities to improve the company's sales and reputation by buying from businesses in underserved markets, he or she would probably respond, "If there were good suppliers in those communities, we would already be buying from them. If we're not buying from them, it's because they can't meet our requirements for quality, cost, service, and stability. But thanks for your input nonetheless."

This manager would be both right and wrong. *Right,* in that most purchasing departments have succeeded in finding competent vendors who can deliver high-quality goods on time at a competitive price. And those vendors are drawn from a wide variety of communities, some mainstream and some underserved.

But also wrong, because there are specific strategies for purchasing in ways that help to increase sales, build customer loyalty, and insulate against risks to brand and reputation. Most purchasing occurs without employing these strategies. This chapter focuses on three such strategies, showing how to improve your company's ability to develop new suppliers from underserved communities and to change the relationship with existing suppliers, in ways that create value both for your business and for the communities.

UNDERSTANDING THE CHALLENGE OF PURCHASING IN A GLOBALIZED ECONOMY

No matter what your business is, odds are that it already purchases goods and services produced in underserved communities. Economic globalization has increased dramatically over the past 50 years, with the average increase in global trade being roughly double the average increase in the global GDP over this period. But economic globalization is not new—business has been globalizing since before Columbus, driven by a search for new sources of raw materials, new markets, and low-cost labor. What's different now? One new aspect is the global reach of business "watchdogs." Although some nonprofit organizations would like to partner with businesses, others are firmly convinced that businesses are the source of many of today's problems—and should be brought to task.

Activist nonprofits, students, unions, and the media are closely scrutinizing today's global corporations. They are empowered with the means (especially with the advent of the Internet and 24/7 news channels) to affect your company's reputation. Since the World Trade Organization's meeting in 1999 in Seattle, an anti-globalization movement has emerged as a potent force. Comprised of groups from around the world with wide-ranging concerns about the environment, human rights, labor rights, and many others, the movement sees business as part of the problem. Companies like Coca-Cola, Newmont Mining, Home Depot, Nike, McDonald's, Shell, and Wal-Mart know all too well that it may only take one person with a computer, an activist nonprofit on a shoestring budget, or a small rural community to be the "mouse that roars," creating long-term negative effects on a company's reputation. This means that how you purchase, and the practices of companies in your supply chain, can have an effect on your reputation.

Indeed, your reputation is more important today than ever before. According to a 2004 report prepared by Arthur D. Little for the World Economic Forum, "Reputation is critical for corporate success, topping the intangible asset list of most CEOs" (Arthur D. Little, 2003). In fact, intangible assets like reputation have become the primary source of shareholder value. For example, as of September 2005 the average S&P 500 price-to-book ratio is 2.85, demonstrating that intangible assets—such as brand, intellectual property, knowledge and human capital, innovation capability, customer loyalty and reputation—were valued at almost three times tangible assets.

An increasingly important factor in a company's reputation is its social and environmental responsibility. According to the *Millennium Poll* published in 1999 by Environics International (now Globescan) perceptions of company reputations are more strongly linked with corporate citizenship (56%) than either brand quality (40%) or perceptions of business management (34%) (Environics, 1999, 2002). According to a 2002 Cone Corporate Citizenship Study, nearly 80 percent of Americans believe companies have a social responsibility. In addition, 75 percent of the survey respondents said that if they learned about a company's negative social practices, they would consider boycotting that company's products or switching to another company's products or services (Cone, Inc., 2002). According to a study completed by APCO Worldwide in 2004 of opinion elite (representing the top 10% of society in terms of media consumption, civic engagement, and interest in public policy issues), 72 percent of opinion elites have purchased a company's products and services and 61 percent have recommended the company to others in response to positive corporate social responsibility (CSR) information. Moreover, negative news also influences their behavior—60 percent of opinion elites have boycotted a company's products and services in response to negative CSR news (Apco Worldwide, 2004).

Activist consumers express their values in a variety of ways. The retail consumer uses boycotts or ethical purchasing, while the institutional consumer (like a government) may set certain requirements (local sourcing, allocations to minority businesses, etc.). The message is clear: building trust and respect with stakeholders and demonstrating corporate responsibility with consumers are now critical to maintaining the license to operate around the world. And supply chain management has become a crucial battleground for building or destroying corporate reputation based on perceptions of corporate irresponsibility.

CREATING VALUE IN THE SUPPLY CHAIN

If you only remember one thing from this chapter, it should be this: creating value through the supply chain is about how to improve sales and reduce risks to brand by changing purchasing practices. It is not about how to reduce the cost per unit for purchased items or how to reduce the costs associated with running the purchasing function.

The strategies highlighted in this section help improve sales and reduce risks to brand, so they are typically popular with managers in sales, marketing, and corporate reputation, because they will help them achieve their goals. They also create benefits for communities, so they are popular with both community residents and the corporate community relations team. But frankly, these strategies are not always as welcome to purchasing managers, because they make purchasing more complex and challenging. In the long run, they increase the strategic value of purchasing. But in the short run, they can create headaches for the purchasing manager.

Once you understand this, you will also understand immediately why increasing value in the supply chain requires a cross-departmental approach and why that approach needs to be supported by top management. This is about how the company as a whole benefits, and it requires close coordination among functions. It also requires management to change some of the incentives for the purchasing function and the way its performance is measured, because the purchasing function will be engaging in a more complex set of tasks.

What are the ways to shape purchasing to increase sales and customer loyalty, and to reduce risks to reputation? There are three broad approaches:

1. *Use "Fair Trade" purchasing to differentiate products and increase sales.* Companies have discovered that they can increase their sales by purchasing some of their supplies on a Fair Trade basis and using the Fair Trade label as part of their brand. The Fair Trade certification assures consumers that the products were purchased under terms that allow the sellers—typically, small producers in underserved markets—to earn a decent living. Companies have used the Fair Trade label to create niche products that have been successfully differentiated from their competition, and thereby increased sales and profits. Fair Trade also creates measurable benefits for small farmers in underserved communities, including increased income and better access to markets.

2. *Use "Targeted Purchasing" to increase customer loyalty and sales.*
   Targeted Purchasing involves directing a portion of a company's
   purchasing to vendors located in a specific community, or owned
   and operated by members of a specific group. In the United States,
   this approach may involve purchasing from minority-owned businesses or women-owned businesses for example. There is persuasive evidence that customer loyalty and sales can be increased
   significantly in specific customer segments through targeted purchasing (Asaba Group, 2005). Targeted purchasing can also be
   used to develop new products for underserved markets and to
   improve community relationships and reduce security problems.

3. *Adopt auditable international standards to protect brand and reputation.* Sometime soon, you are likely to be held responsible by your
   customers for the behaviors of your suppliers—their labor practices, their environmental practices, and their human rights practices. Even though it may not be fair or reasonable to hold you
   responsible for activities that occur in factories you don't control,
   managed by people who don't report to you, customers will do so.
   Auditable international standards and management systems that
   support and enforce these standards are the key to protecting your
   brand and reputation. This is critically important in many underserved communities, where government oversight and control of
   labor, environmental, and human rights practices may not meet
   the standards of customers in all parts of the developed world.

1. Use "Fair Trade" Purchasing to Differentiate Products and Increase Sales

"Fair Trade" purchasing today primarily focuses on agricultural communities, which are an important export from underserved communities. But as the name implies, "agricultural commodities" typically have
no way to be differentiated. Each producer's products are treated the
same way in the marketplace. Companies are finding that there is a
new way to differentiate these products, and their own products, by
changing the basis on which commodities are purchased and using
that basis to create new products and sales. Coffee is an example of an
agricultural commodity for which it has been possible to develop benefits for both companies and communities by changing the purchasing

paradigm. In the standard paradigm, the price for coffee is set on the open market, with all beans of a similar-quality grade priced in a similar way. While this approach has generated consistent pricing and quality across the international market, the recent slump in coffee prices has highlighted the fact that many growers of beans, especially small family farms, are facing economic ruin. This situation has led to the development of Fair Trade certified coffees, which are purchased in ways that enable coffee growers to be economically sustainable. All coffee purchased under the Fair Trade certified standard meets the following requirements:

- The farmers are paid a price that enables them to sustain their operations (in 2004, the price was $1.26 per pound, which was 75 to 100% above world prices).
- The farmers trade directly with importers and roasters in the country where the coffee is consumed.
- The farmers have access to credit and technical assistance in growing coffee in environmentally sustainable ways.

This standard was developed and is maintained by Fairtrade Labeling Organizations International (FLO), a consortium of Fair Trade organizations in Japan, Canada, the United States, and 17 European countries. FLO makes annual inspection visits to producer groups on its Fair Trade register to ensure that the benefits of Fair Trade are reaching producers. In addition to ground-level inspections, FLO inspectors review financial documents and Fair Trade transactions of each producer group. This ensures that the financial benefits are flowing through to the farmers, essentially all of whom are low-income individuals in developing countries.

Companies have been able to use the Fair Trade certified standard to differentiate their coffee from other coffees that are not Fair Trade certified. More important, they are able to increase the price for Fair Trade certified coffee enough to more than offset the additional cost. Coffee companies marketing Fair Trade certified coffee have been able to increase their sales and profits while at the same time helping to improve the income of coffee-producing farmers. The growth in Fair Trade certified coffee and other products has been dramatic, rising from 25,972 metric tons in 1997 to 125,596 metric tons in 2004—a growth of 480 percent over 8 years (Fairtrade Labeling Organizations International, 2006).

2. Use "Targeted Purchasing" to Increase Customer Loyalty and Sales

Targeted purchasing involves the directing of purchasing dollars to specific communities. Companies may set targets for the dollar amount, or the percentage, of their purchasing that they seek to obtain from particular communities, regions, or ethnic groups. Why do businesses target their purchasing?

To Increase Customer Loyalty and Gain Sales. Some customer segments are concerned about where and how a company sources its products. They look to see whether the company is sourcing from groups that they care about—often companies in their region, or companies owned by members of their ethnic, racial, or gender group. For example, DaimlerChrysler has made purchasing from minority communities in the United States a major element of its supplier program, because it has solid data showing that members of minority communities consider its purchasing track record as part of their own purchasing decisions. As a result, the company's total spending on minority suppliers grew from $1 billion in 1999 to $3 billion in 2004—roughly 11 percent of the total supplier purchasing for DaimlerChrysler in the United States (Lester-Miller, 2004). In addition, in many parts of the world there are regulations requiring local content in manufacturing, or requiring joint ventures with local companies as a part of doing business. This is particularly true for products and services purchased by governmental agencies. Many companies have developed specific programs for creating supplier relationships to meet these regulatory requirements.

To Increase Sales in New Markets. Companies, particularly those that serve retail markets in fashion, food, and lifestyle segments, sometimes use their purchasing relationships to gain insight into market segments and to develop innovative products to meet the needs of these consumers. For example, Kroger Supermarkets worked closely with an existing vendor, Glory Foods, a black-owned business that specializes in "Southern Style" canned and frozen foods. Through this purchasing relationship, it was able to develop the "Kroger Southern Selections" line of frozen entrees and side dishes. Kroger had realized that there was a market for southern-style frozen dinners, and it had no entry for this market among its corporate-brand frozen food assortment. It already had a productive relationship with Glory Foods and felt that its experience in this market could help Kroger to successfully develop a niche line. Featuring both company logos on the package, the line "celebrates the time-honored tradition of slow-simmered, down-home Southern cooking," such as Black Bean & Sausage Bake, Potatoes & Vegetables, and Sweet Corn Pudding. The line was launched in 2003, and sales came in at 25 percent ahead of projections. Additional items are being added to the line now (National Minority Supplier Development Council, 2005a).

To Improve Community Relations/Security. Companies that operate large facilities in underserved communities often seek to purchase from local businesses as a way of improving community relations and reducing security concerns. This is particularly true for facilities that do not employ large numbers of local residents, such as plants in the extractive industries. For example, Shell has made significant efforts to increase local purchasing in Nigeria. It purchased its first "made-in-Nigeria" flowstation (a major capital component in its plant) in 2003. It has changed its tendering criteria to require its foreign bidders to work with indigenous contractors. These activities, as well as others, helped to cut the percentage of "community incidents" leading to production shortfalls roughly in half from 1999 to 2003 (Shell Petroleum Company of Nigeria, 2003).

3. Adopt Auditable International Standards to Protect Brand and Reputation

Many companies today are participating in the development of auditable international standards for the treatment of workers, for environmental protection, and for human rights. To understand why, it can be helpful to review the context. In today's globalized economy, supply chains stretch across the world. Some of your suppliers are in areas where the laws regarding human rights, environmental protection, and workplace safety and protection are quite different from the laws in countries where many of your customers live and work. Simply ensuring that your suppliers are complying with the laws and regulations of their country isn't enough to guarantee that your customers will always be satisfied that conditions in your supply chain meet their expectations.

There are many well-known examples of situations where the failure to meet customer expectations led to significant problems for companies. In the area of apparel and footwear, the problems that Nike faced due to poor working conditions and environmental problems with factories in its supply chain in Vietnam are well known. Kathie Lee Gifford's problems with "sweat-shop" conditions in the factories making her trademarked line of clothing provide another high-profile example.

Many companies have addressed this problem by developing their own codes of conduct for the treatment of workers, environmental safety, and human rights. In order for a vendor to become or continue to be a supplier for the company, it has to agree to adhere to the code of conduct in its operations. Many codes also require that the supplier have some type of yearly third-party audit to ensure that full compliance is occurring.

While this approach makes sense, as the number of companies that developed their own codes of conduct multiplied, the cost to companies and suppliers also multiplied. Consider the case of Toys "R" Us. This company buys products manufactured in approximately 20,000 factories. If all subcontractors are included, there are over 110,000 businesses that Toys "R" Us purchases from. A serious problem with workplace safety or environmental standards in any one of these could pose a threat to the Toys "R" Us brand and reputation. And yet, the cost of getting each one of these businesses to commit to adhering to the Toys "R" Us code of conduct, and then monitoring them all for compliance, would be huge (Deluca, 2003).

There are also significant costs for vendors. Toys "R" Us is not the only company that purchases from them which has developed a code of conduct. In fact, as of 2003, 60 percent of the Fortune 500 had developed codes of conduct for their suppliers. This means that, as of 2003, there were 300 different codes in place among the Fortune 500. What makes this particularly challenging for many suppliers is that they supply not one, but many large companies. This means that there might be ten, twenty, or thirty different codes of conduct that they need to follow in order to remain suppliers to their various cus-

---

Management Tips: Codes of Conduct

Codes of conduct for supplies should spell out the company's expectations regarding:

- prohibition of child labor
- adherence to local labor laws
- requirements for working conditions
- assurance of workers' freedom of association
- prohibition of forced labor
- prohibition of discrimination
- requirements for wages and work hours
- environmental practices and policies

Source: Gap, 2005.

---

tomers. And the codes don't all agree. Suppliers also need to have ten, twenty, or thirty different audit teams in their factories each year to certify that they are adhering to the various codes. Clearly, this situation is not efficient for either the purchasers or the suppliers.

The solution involves auditable international standards for the treatment of workers, for environmental protection, and for human rights. These standards are similar to the ISO9000 quality standard, which provides an internationally agreed-upon approach to measuring quality and a management system that helps integrate quality into the day-to-day operations of a company. In a similar way, environmental standards such as ISO14000 and workplace standards such as SA8000 provide internationally recognized measures that can satisfy purchasers and customers alike that appropriate standards are being met. It also enables suppliers to have just one uniform set of standards to which they must adhere, as well as just one audit team that they need to satisfy. This system creates benefits for businesses because it provides a cost-effective, verifiable way for ensuring that brand and reputation can be defended from attack due to alleged abuses in its supply chain. It creates benefits for vendors because it provides one clear standard that they can strive to comply with. It creates benefits for communities because it helps to improve the conditions in the factories in which their members work. See the box above for tips from the Gap and others on important elements of a code of conduct.

CREATING VALUE IN THE SUPPLY CHAIN

Even though there are three different strategies for increasing sales and protecting brand through purchasing from underserved communities, the five success factors apply to all. This section shows how managers can implement the success factors, no matter which of the three strategies they are using, to create value in the supply chain.

▪ I. MINE AND TRANSLATE LOCAL MARKET INFORMATION

What's Different about Underserved Markets

Purchasing from underserved communities can help your company to increase sales and reduce risks to brand and reputation. But these benefits are unlikely to occur if you rely on the standard sources of information about your suppliers. Standard sources provide excellent information about suppliers in mainstream markets. These sources also furnish information on suppliers in underserved communities and countries. But they can't help you determine how well these suppliers may be able to serve your company in improving sales and protecting brand, no matter which strategies for creating value through the supply chain you follow.

What to Do in Underserved Markets

You'll need to turn to new types of brokers and certification organizations. These entities can help your business to mine and translate local market information—specifically, information about potential suppliers in underserved markets. The specific types of organizations vary, depending on which of the three strategies your company is pursuing. But in general, they can be divided into two types: (1) independent, third-party certification organizations, and (2) purchasing brokers.

Use Independent Certification Organizations

Independent certification is a well-established practice throughout the business world. In most areas of certification, there are both standard-

What's different?

- Existing business networks don't do a good job of helping businesses to find vendors from underserved communities that meet their requirements.

What to do about it.

- Use independent certification organizations to efficiently determine whether vendors meet company and customers standards.
- Use purchasing brokers to identify and help build productive relationships with vendors in underserved communities.

setting organizations and certifying organizations. Consider, for example, materials quality. One of the leading standard-setting organizations in the field of materials quality is ASTM International (formerly the American Society for Testing and Materials). ASTM International is a voluntary international organization that develops consensus-based standards for materials and processes. It has over 30,000 members and maintains standards for more than 12,000 different materials and processes. As a standard-setting body, ASTM International *develops* standards but does not *certify* that specific products meet those standards. That is the job of the certifying organizations. One example of a certifying organization is Construction Testing Laboratories (CTL), an independent subsidiary of the Portland Cement Association. CTL offers testing and certification services for a wide range of building products, including wall, roof, and floor panels and beams; masonry blocks and assemblies; anchors and fasteners; reinforced and pre-stressed pipes; and concrete materials. CTL develops and implements test programs to help manufacturers gain building-code acceptance for their products.

Just as there are standard-setting and certifying organizations for mainstream products and markets, there are standard-setting and certifying organizations for underserved markets. Social Accountability International (SAI) is an example of a standard-setting organization in the area of factory operations and workforce standards. SAI convenes all key stakeholders, including companies, government agencies, nongovernmental organizations, workers and trade unions, socially responsible investors, and consumers, to develop consensus-based voluntary standards. Through this process, it has developed SA8000, a tool for retailers, brand companies, suppliers, and other organizations to ensure humane working conditions in the supply chain. This standard helps companies make sure that their suppliers are treating their workforce in a manner that complies with all major labor conventions, and that there is no child labor in the supply chain. By ensuring that all suppliers are in compliance with the standard, a company can protect its brand and reputation from attacks by activists claiming unfair treatment of workers or inhumane working conditions in the supply chain. The SA8000 standard has been adopted by companies with sales totaling more than $100 billion, including Avon Products, Dole Food, Eileen Fisher, Gap, Synergies Worldwide, Timberland, Toys "R" Us, and Vögele Mode.

SAI also accredits certifying organizations that visit factories in the supply chain to ensure that they are in compliance with the SA8000 standard. If they are not, then the management is required to develop a plan for coming into compliance that is approved by the certifying organization.

TransFair USA is an example of a certifying organization in the area of fair trade. TransFair USA has been accredited by Fairtrade Labeling Organizations (FLO), the standard-setting body for fair trade. TransFair USA is the only independent third-party certification organization for fair trade in the United States; it certifies coffee, tea, bananas, cocoa, and other products. TransFair plays three critical roles for its business partners:

- *Certification.* TransFair audits the global supply chain from the producers to the U.S. buyers and distributors, and it licenses companies to display the trademarked Fair Trade Certified label on products that meet Fair Trade criteria.
- *Business development.* TransFair develops PR and marketing programs to help companies promote their Fair Trade products.
- *Consumer awareness.* TransFair actively partners with environmental, faith-based, student, and consumer organizations to generate grassroots consumer demand and promotional support for Fair Trade products on a national level.

Through these activities, TransFair has helped to spur a sharp increase in the demand for fair-trade goods. For example, the number of pounds of coffee certified as Fair Trade in the United States surged from 9.7 million pounds in 2002 to 32.8 million in 2004. Dunkin' Donuts is projecting that it will serve 30 million Fair Trade lattes and cappuccinos in 2005 alone (TransFair USA, 2005).

Use Purchasing Brokers

Companies use brokering organizations to help them efficiently find potential suppliers in underserved communities and to determine whether those suppliers can meet their needs for quality, price, and service. The National Minority Supplier Development Council (NMSDC) is one of the largest and best-known brokering organizations in the United States. It helps to connect Fortune 500 companies with well-established and well-run minority-owned companies that can serve as vendors. NMSDC is a membership organization, created by the major purchasing companies to help them meet their needs for high-quality, reliable, and easy access to minority-owned firms. The NMSDC Network includes a National Office in New York and 39 regional councils across the country. There are 3,500 corporate members throughout the network, including most of America's largest publicly owned, privately owned, and foreign-owned companies, as well as universities, hospitals, and other buying institutions. The regional councils certify and match more than 15,000 minority-owned businesses with member corporations that want to purchase goods and services.

NMSDC's services include the following:

1. *Certification.* NMSDC has developed fair and standard procedures to ensure consistent and identical review and certification of minority-owned businesses. These businesses are certified by NMSDC's affiliate nearest to the company's headquarters.
2. *Database.* NMSDC maintains a national database that provides comprehensive information on more than 15,000 of America's top minority-owned firms. The information is collected by NMSDC's regional councils and is available only to NMSDC members.
3. *Financing.* Through its Business Consortium Fund and its Growth Initiative, NMSDC can provide both debt and equity financing to minority-owned firms that show the potential for significant growth.
4. *Education.* In partnership with the Kellogg Graduate School of Management at Northwestern University, NMSDC offers an Advanced Management Education Program to provide certified,

established, expansion-oriented Minority Business Enterprises (MBEs) with the tools and skills needed to achieve and sustain accelerated growth.

In part through NMSDC's work, purchasing by major corporations from minority-owned businesses roughly doubled from 1998 to 2003, growing from $41.0 billion to $80.2 billion (National Minority Supplier Development Council, 2005a).

▪ 2. ADAPT BUSINESS MODEL TO COMMUNITY REALITIES

What's Different about Underserved Markets

Even though purchasing from underserved markets can be helpful to sales and brand, it is not always easy to accomplish. Many vendors from underserved markets that would give the most benefit to a purchaser's sales or reputation are too small, or too inexperienced, or too financially fragile, to meet all of a multinational corporation's purchasing requirements. In order to purchase from them, it is sometimes necessary to help them develop into solid, efficient, and stable suppliers.

But why would a major company bother to do this? Why not just purchase from existing suppliers, rather than go through the difficulty of developing new suppliers in underserved markets? *Because the benefit to sales, community relations, and brand and reputation is worth the additional cost.*

This shift from purchasing to development and purchasing is a major change in the business model for purchasing for most corporations. It moves purchasing from a transactional basis to something that looks more like a long-term partnership between corporation and supplier. It's more expensive and time-consuming

What's different?

- Vendors/distributors don't have the complete set of technical skills, quality control, and financial depth that purchasers require.

What to do about it.

- Create skills transfer programs and opportunities.
- Use purchasing requirements to motivate change in suppliers.
- Create financing mechanisms to enable growth and stability.

than the standard approach to purchasing. And it's worth doing only when the payoff to the company is significant. When this is the case, there are three major approaches to the development of suppliers: (1) transfer skills to suppliers, (2) use purchasing requirements to motivate change in suppliers, and (3) create financing mechanisms to promote growth and stability.

What to Do in Underserved Markets

Transfer Skills to Suppliers

Sourcing locally can often be difficult because of existing and available suppliers' inability to keep up with a company's demand. One solution is to transfer skills to suppliers so that they can produce at necessary levels through technology and training. Baileys Ireland, a subsidiary of the international drinks company Diageo, has utilized this approach to meet demands for locally sourced cream, an essential ingredient in its Baileys Irish Cream Liqueur.

Since the drink's launch in the 1970s, Baileys Irish Cream Liqueur has become the world's biggest-selling cream liqueur. Initially, the company was able to source the cream required for production from the surplus of Dublin's domestic milk market. But due to rapid growth, Baileys' need for cream equaled the entire Dublin market by 1998. The company wanted to maintain the brand as authentically Irish so was reluctant to look outside of the country to source its cream. However, the Irish dairy market was fragmented into small farms, causing low output rates. Baileys knew that to continue sourcing locally, it would have to increase the skills and capacity of the market players. Local dairy farmers would need technical capabilities and management training.

The company responded to this dilemma in a variety of ways. It helped to modernize the local dairy market by (1) assisting in identifying key needs for introducing modern farming techniques, (2) arranging for new technologies to be introduced to small dairy farmers, (3) commissioning specialists to train farmers in new management principles and practices, and (4) helping introduce a quality control system to farms that would ensure a consistent supply of high-quality cream. The company's initiative was successful, and Irish farmers now produce enough cream to satisfy Baileys' production needs.

The transfer of skills and know-how in the dairy market in Ireland has allowed Baileys to sustain the Irish element as an important part of its brand. More important, it has enabled the company to continue to source locally and further contribute to the national agricultural economy. As a result of the initiative, annual milk production has increased in Ireland and more than 3,000 small farmers have gained access to training and new technologies that have grown their businesses (International Business Leaders Forum, 2002).

Use Purchasing Requirements to Motivate Change in Suppliers

Large companies can use their purchasing power to encourage their suppliers to change their operations and improve their quality, reliability, and stability. For example, the Ford Motor Company has used its purchasing power to encourage its primary suppliers (the "Tier 1 suppliers") to start their own targeted purchasing programs ("Tier 2 programs"). In 2004, Ford Motor Company's Supplier Diversity Development (SDD) department launched an Internet-based reporting program called the M-Tier Diversity Reporting System. The purpose/vision of M-Tier is twofold: (1) to capture minority purchasing at all levels of Ford's value chain, and (2) to assist suppliers in Ford's value chain with the initiation of their own Tier 2 reporting programs. Ford is particularly interested in helping assist suppliers "without background, experience or financial capability" to start their own Tier 2 programs. All of the data in the system will roll up into a company-wide report that will allow Ford to provide a comprehensive picture of the purchasing from minority-owned firms throughout its supply chain.

The system also enables Ford to track the performance of each of its suppliers in minority purchasing. Ford uses this information to provide incentives for increased performance. Ford notes on the M-Tier Web site for suppliers,

Based on your most recent report, your Tier 2 minority sourcing status is either Red, Yellow or Green. Your Tier 2 minority sourcing status is reviewed by your Ford buyer and SDD business manager. Our process stipulates that our Red suppliers meet with their Supplier Diversity Business Manager/Buyer/Purchasing

Manager/Director to develop a roadmap to improve your performance. Although there is no immediate consequence associated with the rating, Tier 2 performance is considered during sourcing decisions and is used as a filter for consideration for various Ford awards, such as our World Excellence Awards and SDD Corporate Citizenship Award.

Ford also provides technical assistance to minority-owned businesses in its supply chain. In 1997, the VP of Purchasing at Ford recognized a need for new initiatives to increase the company's long-standing commitment to doing business with minority suppliers. While Ford had had an active minority purchasing program since the 1960s, many minority suppliers were still not able to meet all the company's requirements. The company also was seeing much of its talented workforce walk out of the door and into retirement. The retirees' talent and expertise were what many of the company's minority suppliers needed. Pulling these two together was the inception of Ford's Technical Assistance Program.

The first supplier to take advantage of the program was Ideal Steel, which lacked the capacity to paint the steel it supplied the company in an effective manner, creating a bottleneck in the supply chain. Ford sent a retired engineer from its paint systems division to train workers at Ideal Steel. Within a few weeks, the supplier increased its throughput by 100 percent.

The Technical Assistance Program has since helped hundreds of Ford suppliers with issues from manufacturing bottlenecks to ISO certification. The focus is on development; Ford is helping its suppliers develop new skills while the company has developed a more efficient supply chain (Ford Motor Company, 2005; Hines and Larson, 2005).

Create Financing Mechanisms to Promote Growth and Stability

One of the most successful examples of financing mechanisms that provides support to suppliers of major corporations is the NMSDC Business Consortium Fund. The Business Consortium Fund (BCF) provides loans to NMSDC-certified businesses that have supplier/vendor relationships with national or local corporate members, through a network of participating banks. The BCF and its subsidiaries offer a wide range of financing vehicles, including working capital loans, term loans, equipment financing, accounts receivable financing, equipment leasing, long-term mezzanine financing, and financial advisory services, in addition to traditional contract and purchase order financing products. The BCF will consider purchasing a loan participation or extending a loan guarantee for up to 75 percent of the loan amount. In each case, the maximum retained risk for the BCF is $750,000 and $562,500, respectively.

The Business Consortium Fund is a nonprofit arm of NMSDC that is funded primarily through investments and contributions made by NMSDC corporate members and other organizations. Since 1986, BCF Investors & Contributors have provided more than $22 million in capital to the BCF. These firms invested in the BCF because they understand that minority business development goes beyond having a supplier diversity program. Their funding enables the BCF to fulfill its mission to provide access to capital to NMSDC-certified firms that experience difficulty obtaining financing on reasonable terms through conventional channels. As a result of sharing in the risk undertaken by participating lenders by way of credit enhancement, the BCF makes loans possible that would not otherwise be made based on the lenders' traditional underwriting standards. From inception through the end of 2004, the BCF extended more than $180 million in loans and/or guarantees to approximately 725 MBEs, creating more than 7,000 jobs (National Minority Supplier Development Council, 2005b).

■ 3. CHANGE INTERNAL INCENTIVES AND CHALLENGE CULTURAL ASSUMPTIONS

What's Different about Underserved Markets

There are many examples of companies that have made public commitments to purchasing or hiring from underserved communities and that have launched their programs with great fanfare. But a careful review of these examples several years later sometimes shows that little progress has been made. Why do some programs, even those with support from top management, achieve so little, while others make significant strides?

What's different?

- Business "silos" prevent companies from seeing total value to purchasing from underserved communities.
- Mistaken beliefs/prejudices prevent managers from embracing purchasing from underserved communities.

What to do about it.

- Create cross-functional teams to generate understanding of "whole corporation" benefit.
- Create internal incentives to expand purchasing from underserved markets.
- Build networking opportunities to enable personal contact and connections.

Part of the answer lies in whether management has spent time and energy mapping out the existing corporate culture and structures, and designing and implementing the changes required to enable new purchasing strategies to succeed. When purchasing programs fail, they often fail for one of the following reasons:

Too Narrow a View of Benefits. As we noted at the beginning of this chapter, the value to purchasing from underserved markets typically is distributed across several functions—sales, community relations, reputation management, and the like. But the cost is often borne primarily by the purchasing unit. If no attempt is made to understand and measure the benefits across several "silos," it is likely that the purchasing function will "underinvest" in the programs, since it sees all of the costs but only a limited part of the benefits.

Misaligned Incentives. Most corporate purchasing units have clearly defined incentives, which include acquiring high-quality products at the lowest competitive price with limited time and resources. When purchasing from underserved communities, it can take more time and energy to get the same level of quality and price as purchasing from existing suppliers. If the incentives for the purchasing department's staff don't explicitly reward them for purchasing from underserved communities and provide them with the support needed to do so well, it is unlikely that they will invest the time and energy required to help the program to grow.

Mistaken Beliefs/Prejudices. Managers who are not members of underserved markets may have mistaken beliefs about the value or the difficulty of doing business with these markets. While there may in fact be some additional cost or risk, their beliefs may significantly exaggerate those factors. Managers also may have prejudices against members of communities in underserved markets. All of these issues preclude them from investing time and energy in developing supplier relationships in underserved markets.

What to Do in Underserved Markets

In order to ensure the long-term success and viability of the purchasing program, a manager must embed it within the culture and operations of the corporation. He or she must change internal incentives, align organizational structures, and challenge cultural assumptions. The key strategies are the following:

Create Cross-functional Teams. The benefit of purchasing from underserved markets covers multiple functions. One strategy for ensuring that this benefit is captured and maximized is to create a team that includes representatives from the functions that will gain the benefits, as well as from the functions that are centrally involved in making the purchase decision. The functions that gain the benefits will provide the energy, championing the efforts that need to be made. The functions that have to make it happen will provide some balance, forcing the team to prioritize and set goals and targets. Together, both sides will drive the organization to a solid and cost-efficient program.

Align Behavioral Incentives. One truism of corporate design is that behavior is driven by incentives. If you are trying to introduce a new program demanding new behaviors, and you don't change any of the existing incentives, you are likely to find a fairly weak response. It is important to look carefully at all the incentives in place and to determine how to tweak them so that purchasing from underserved markets will be encouraged rather than dampened. This is particularly true in situations where the purchasing requires supplier development, not just supplier identification and certification.

Build Networking Opportunities. Communication and trust are important parts of any business relationship, and purchasing is no different. If the purchasing agents don't understand or trust suppliers from underserved markets, they will have a harder time making the relationship work well. It is important to build opportunities for purchasing agents to develop contact with potential suppliers before the moment comes to solicit a proposal. It is particularly useful if this can occur in a context that allows the purchasing managers to get reliable information about the suppliers from peers whom they trust and respect.

The following examples show in detail how certain companies have implemented these approaches.

Create Cross-functional Teams

Texas Instruments' experience illustrates the importance of cross-functional teams and of internal incentives in helping to enable the success of a diversity marketing initiative. Until the late 1980s, Texas Instruments (TI) was largely focused on providing solutions for the defense industry, which required companies to purchase a portion of its business needs from minority- and women-owned suppliers. TI became a leader in developing ways to meet and exceed this goal. By 1989, TI was no longer in the defense business and thus no longer tied to the federal requirements. However, a new challenge emerged that caused TI to revisit its experience with minority and women business development. A lack of economic parity for the minority community in the Dallas, Texas, area—where 30 percent of TI's employees work and live—had resulted in tension and unrest in the city. The situation presented a real business threat to TI and other area businesses. If the threat was ignored, the community infrastructure and quality of life would suffer, and along with it, TI's ability to retain and attract a skilled and dependable workforce and supplier base in the Dallas area. With a strong conviction that area businesses should be part of developing a solution, TI revived and expanded its former Minority/Women Business Development (M/WBD) program to serve the Dallas area specifically, and to include sourcing of product throughout all commercial operations company-wide.

To ensure that the program would be successful, TI created a strong cross-functional team charged with implementing it. The head of the M/WBD program reports directly to the vice president of procurement and logistics. There are seven positions within the

M/WBD team, which manages all aspects of the M/WBD program and is charged with the program's direction and success. The team's goals are to:

- identify, assist, and develop minority and women suppliers to become qualified suppliers to TI;
- encourage purchases from minority and women suppliers, particularly in communities where TI has a presence;
- conduct formal and timely reviews of progress against its own goals for procurement from minority- and women-owned businesses.

The team coordinates and assists in all domestic procurement from minority- and women-owned businesses. It is the first point of contact for all minority- and women-owned businesses seeking advice and guidance.

Align Behavioral Incentives

In addition to developing a cross-functional team charged with implementing the program, TI established an internal incentive program that motivated TI employees to achieve the program's goals. The Contract Bonus Plan gives each director in procurement and logistics up to $3,500 to give cash rewards to employees who most successfully promote the development of new or increased procurements from minority- and women-owned businesses. The incentive is also available to employees in Supplier Sourcing in the M/WBD team.

The process begins with the selection of 20 minority suppliers who have the greatest potential for increased business development for commodities or services. M/WBD staff select these suppliers based upon supplier feedback, the staff's knowledge of services, and overall capability. Then, strategy teams for each supplier are established—typically consisting of the purchasing agents, M/WBD staff, operations personnel, and the supplier. The team identifies potential services the supplier may be able to provide or expand, and then it defines the obstacles that may restrict the supplier from providing the selected services or commodities. A plan is developed and implemented to best ensure supplier success. The Contract Bonus Plan has been highly successful. In one year, the selected suppliers increased their business with TI by 40 percent over the previous year. These companies accounted for the majority of the procurements from minority- and women-owned businesses for the company. Over ten years, TI was able to increase its purchases from minority- and women-owned businesses to the point where they constituted 5 percent of the total domestic TI purchasing in 2004 (Center for Corporate Citizenship, 2001; Texas Instruments, 2005).

Build Networking Opportunities

DaimlerChrysler Corporation purchases approximately $3 billion per year from minority-owned businesses, roughly 11 percent of its total purchasing. One of DaimlerChrysler's strategies for achieving this result is to host an annual Automotive Matchmaker event. This event draws over a thousand people, who participate in intensive networking and education, from over 400 minority-owned businesses, Tier 1 suppliers, Original Equipment Manufacturer (OEM) customers, and Chrysler itself. Chrysler estimates that over five years, its annual Matchmaker conferences have generated more than $500 million in new business for MBEs by enabling Chrysler team members, customers, and a wide range of suppliers to meet and learn about each other's respective requirements, goods, and services. Similar networking conferences are held annually by most of the major corporations in the automotive industry and have generated similar results. The opportunity to meet, greet, and learn about other participants in the industry is a key tool for helping to increase sales from underserved markets (Diversity Careers, 2005).

■ 4. CREATE PARTNERSHIPS AND STRATEGIC ALLIANCES

What's Different in Underserved Markets

There are many situations in mainstream markets where it is not cost-effective for a purchasing agent to buy directly from an individual producer. For example, the producer may operate at too small a scale or may be located in an area that is hard to reach. Conversely, the purchasing agent may be buying at too small a scale to get the discounts needed. The purchasing industry has developed a range of institutional arrangements to address these situations. Producers may sell through cooperatives or brokers, who aggregate production from many smaller producers into a lot big enough to sell on the international market. Producers who are too small to have their own sales force may use manufacturer's representatives, who sell products from a wide array of manufacturers. Conversely, purchasers may band together to create joint purchasing programs.

What's different?

- Even though quality and benefits are attractive, specific elements of cost structure make using particular suppliers or reaching particular communities unprofitable.

What to do about it.

- Use partnerships to lower costs and increase benefits for business and community.

The same is true of purchasing from vendors located in underserved communities. There are many cases where it is not cost-effective for a purchasing agent to buy directly from individual producers in these communities. There are also cases where language and cultural barriers make it difficult to develop the understanding and trust that are key to good purchasing relationships.

What to Do in Underserved Markets

Develop Mutually Beneficial Partnerships

As we noted at the beginning of this book, when working in underserved markets, the right partnership can be everything. Often, the key to addressing these difficulties is to create a partnership that makes purchasing more efficient and effective. It is particularly important in working with underserved markets that the partnerships be seen as creating positive economic benefits for both sides. This helps to dispel the suspicion and distrust that residents in underserved communities sometimes have regarding the motives and activities of large companies. These residents believe that large companies have taken advantage of the relative weakness of their communities to negotiate business on unfair terms. Making sure that the partnership is clearly creating benefits for residents can help to address long-standing grievances.

One way that partnerships help to reduce costs and increase benefits is by aggregating supply. Partnerships serve as wholesalers, purchasing products in small amounts from a wide array of individual producers and filling large orders from companies. A more complex approach is to increase quality, timeliness, and volume of production. Partnerships do this by providing producers with training, by grading and certifying the products, and by helping to increase the efficiency of production. Partnerships also can improve the financial viability of producers by supplying working capital to fill orders or by helping to improve the balance sheets of producers.

The strategy of ICICI Bank in providing credit in rural India provides a good example of how a partnership can lower cost and increase demand. The potential market for credit in underserved markets in India is large—over 400 million individuals, most of them rural. Providing banking services for rural farmers and other low-income groups, however, has proven to be difficult for Indian banks. The Indian government, and particularly the regulatory banking arm, the Reserve Bank of India, have long encouraged and mandated banks to tailor their services to this population. However, most banks have approached rural access from a developmental, rather than profit-making, standpoint. In contrast, ICICI Bank, the second-largest bank in India, has come to view this market as having enormous revenue-generating potential.

From the initial steps of extending its banking services to these low-income populations, ICICI Bank approached the initiative as a viable, profit-making venture rather than an experiment to meet government-mandated standards. The company turned its focus to microfinance and self-help groups, an area greatly in need of sustainable solutions as it mostly depends on nonprofit microfinance institutions. (Nonprofit microfinance institutions specialize in making very small loans—as low as $50—to poor individuals in underserved communities.) ICICI Bank's first major step in serving this population was the purchase of the Bank of Madura, which had a significant customer base and 77 branches serving underserved communities. These branches formed the basis for launching banking services for self-help groups—groups of individuals who received loans and collectively guaranteed their repayment. But this strategy only let ICICI Bank efficiently reach customers who lived or worked near the bank branches. Reaching the broad market on a retail basis was too costly for ICICI Bank.

To be able to reach customers in a cost-efficient way, ICICI Bank established a national partnership with the microfinance institutions that already provide loans to underserved communities. ICICI Bank did this by creating, in effect, a secondary market for the loans originated by the microfinance institutions. Under this national partnership, the microfinance institutions originate the loans and service the loan portfolio. ICICI Bank agrees to purchase the loans from the microfinance institutions, thereby providing the institutions with the capital needed to make future loans. The microfinance institutions and ICICI Bank share the risk of the portfolio, with the microfinance institutions being responsible for the first 10 percent of the losses and ICICI Bank being responsible for any remaining losses. In the largest purchase of microfinance loans as of the end of 2004, ICICI Bank purchased a portfolio of 42,500 loans valued at U.S. $4.3 million from Share Microfin Limited, a microfinance institution.

This partnership is a win-win for both ICICI Bank and the underserved communities. ICICI Bank has been able to rapidly expand its lending activities in a profitable way without having to build an expensive infrastructure. It also has been able to manage the risk of lending to underserved communities. The communities, on the other hand, have gained significant additional access to capital, which has allowed the microfinance institutions to expand their lending in a cost-efficient way. This benefits the underserved communities, which are desperately in need of capital for growth and expansion (ICFA Center for Management Research, 2005).

▪ 5. IMPROVE THE ENABLING ENVIRONMENT

What's Different about Underserved Markets

The enabling environment is the set of institutions, laws, and regulations in which business functions and that enables business to be transacted safely, securely, and efficiently. It includes public sector agencies and courts; the transportation, power, and communications infrastructure; commercial finance and banking; and education,

What's different?

- Enabling environment—finance, transportation, education, regulation, and laws—is inadequate for, or disruptive of, creating vendor relationships.

What to do about it.

- Create coalitions to drive improvements in supplier skills, abilities, and financial capacity.
- Advocate for changes in regulation and law.

healthcare, and social organizations. Businesses that are used to purchasing from suppliers in highly developed markets expect the enabling environment to function reasonably well. There may be some disagreements over how bankruptcy works in a particular country; deliveries may be delayed; there may be occasional power outages. But these are the exception rather than the rule.

Unfortunately, the enabling environment in many underserved markets is often much weaker. There can be significant problems with each of the elements of the enabling environment noted above. Laws and regulations may impede rather than support business transactions. Bribery and corruption may be commonplace in dealing with government officials. The transportation infrastructure may be poor, and communications may be underdeveloped. The banking industry may not be adequate, so that credit is not available for fulfilling orders and facilitating growth. Finally, education and healthcare may be lacking, so that the workforce is inadequate or undertrained. Some of the most difficult conditions exist in the poorest countries. For example, the *Economist* profiled the intolerable road conditions and rampant corruption in Cameroon, which makes transportation particularly difficult. There are very few roads—only 2.6 kilometers of road per 1,000 people in 1995, down from 7.2 km per 1,000 in 1980. The roads are in spectacularly bad condition. In addition, there are frequent roadblocks erected by police to "inspect" traffic, many of which are thinly disguised opportunities to extort bribes for passage. To profile this problem, the *Economist's* journalist hitched a ride on a truck making a delivery from Doula, the main port, to Bertoua, a small town 313 miles away. If the road conditions had been normal, the trip would have taken 20 hours, including an overnight rest stop. As it was, the truck was stopped at 47 roadblocks, and the trip took four days. This transportation infrastructure makes it harder both to sell into these markets and to purchase from them (The Economist, 2002).

What to Do in Underserved Markets

Create Coalitions

Corporations can and do work to improve the enabling environments in underserved communities. One approach is to work in coalitions to drive improvements in supplier skills, abilities, and financial capacity, and in the capacity of the educational system and the financial system supporting suppliers and their workforces. Corporations work together as a group to pressure and to help government officials provide better education and training, and to improve the financial services sector. They also work directly with suppliers to improve their skills and abilities.

For example, the International Business Leaders Forum (IBLF) is helping businesses to form partnerships to create profitable small, medium, and micro enterprises in low-income areas across the world. IBLF encourages larger corporations to create "business linkages" to promote the transfer of business knowledge, skills, and technology to smaller enterprises in low-income and developing areas. Linkages not only offer communities development opportunity but make the environment better for larger corporations as well. Business benefits include enhancing local business climates, developing local skills pools, combating overdependence on one employer, reinforcing reputation, and ensuring license to operate.

IBLF has developed the *Business of Enterprise Sourcebook* to guide companies on the path to developing linkages. The publication discusses the need to support local enterprise, outlines the benefits of enterprise development, describes the resource implications of building business linkages, and sets a roadmap for corporate action. Several profiles of successful supplier development partnerships are included in the report. Examples include:

- The involvement of Richards Bay Minerals in creating the Business Linkage Centre in South Africa. The Centre acts as a link between large companies seeking services and small enterprises that become centre members after a rigorous accreditation process.

- A cross-sector partnership of international sportswear companies, including Adidas, Nike, and the Pentland Group, that is working to improve working conditions in Vietnamese factories. The companies committed to good practice in their supplier factories in order to make the market a friendlier environment for further development (International Business Leaders Forum, 2002).

Advocate for Changes in Laws and Regulations

Corporations also work with governments regarding the laws and regulations supporting trade, making them work better for suppliers, purchasers, and consumers. This can be done in an informal way, where companies provide advice and counsel to government ministers to (1) help to improve the functioning of regulations and bureaucracy, and (2) make it more possible for local suppliers to obtain purchasing contracts with multinational corporations.

Companies can also work in a much more public way. This is important when they need to be seen as publicly united in addressing a complex and difficult issue. Initiatives on bribery and corruption often fall into this category. It is quite difficult for one company to take on this issue single-handedly. If one company fights corruption, it will be sorely handicapped if its competitors do not. Getting all the competitors together to develop a joint policy that they all agree to enforce provides a level playing field on which they can all compete. The development of the Business Principles for Countering Bribery is an example of this kind of joint activity. These principles, published in 2002, are directed by a steering committee whose corporate members include Bombardier, BP, General Electric, ISIS Asset Management, Motorola, Norsk Hydro, Organización Corona, Pfizer, PricewaterhouseCoopers, Rio Tinto, SAP, SGS, Shell, Sika, and Tata Sons Ltd. The steering committee also includes nonprofits, multilateral agencies, and trade union representatives (Transparency International, 2005).

A CAUTIONARY TALE

Purchasing properly can help drive sales and protect reputation. But the technique needs to be used carefully, or it can backfire. The

Body Shop's experience illustrates how a company's efforts can hurt rather than help reputation when purchasing from underserved communities.

The Body Shop began in the mid-1970s as a retailer of fine beauty products. Anita Roddick, the founder of the Body Shop chain, very quickly became a force to be reckoned with in the industry. Her concept was anti-corporate and pro-community. Many Body Shop products were packaged and sold as conscientious alternatives to mass-marketed products that harmed animals or used synthetic materials. Her beauty products carried a social philosophy. She was a pioneer of cause-related marketing and branding according to the social beliefs of her target clientele. The Greenpeace Partnership and the Save the Whales campaign, for example, was a pioneering program that directly connected product and cause. And the business model worked: the Body Shop was franchised all over the world and stock prices rose dramatically.

However, criticism began to arise around whether Body Shop products were truly socially and environmentally friendly: instances of product contamination, claims that the environmental mission was "window dressing," inconsistencies between Roddick's labor rights claims and the company's sourcing policies, weak numbers to support its fair trade initiative, and a drastic reduction in charitable giving percentages. The company's most famous attack came in a 1994 *Business Ethics* article entitled "Shattered Image: Is The Body Shop Too Good to Be True?" This set off a firestorm of controversy, which hurt the Body Shop's reputation as a socially and environmentally conscious retailer and contributed in part to its loss of market share to competitors such as Lush, Origins, and Aveda and a drop in its stock price.

Does this mean that purchasing from underserved markets is ill-advised and unacceptably risky, particularly if it is used to drive sales? Not necessarily. The central reason that the Body Shop was vulnerable to attack was that it had not put in place a systematic and auditable set of standards for environmental and social values in its supply chain before it came under fire. This made it difficult to defend quickly against charges that the company wasn't making good on its high-profile claims. Companies can put into place these systems and thus much more easily deflect criticism. The Body

Shop itself is now a good example. Since 1994, it has developed excellent management and audit systems for its supply chain. Analysts rate the Body Shop's environmental management system as one of the best. The company has been a leader in environmental and social reporting and now produces candid and transparent accounts of ethics within the organization. Most important, its social and environmental claims are guaranteed by an independent, credible auditor specializing in providing assurance in environmental health, safety, training, and corporate reporting. The Body Shop has recovered from its earlier problems and, as of 2005, has shown three consecutive years of growth in sales, profitability, and cash flow (Entine, 2002; The Body Shop, 2005).

MEASURING PROGRESS

What measures can help you track and manage purchasing from underserved communities? Purchasing professionals have developed a wide range of measures to understand and direct their purchasing activities. Obviously, they look at price, features, quality, reliability, and delivery time. But they also look at the indicators of the strength of their suppliers, the ability to manage fluctuations in demand, and the ability to integrate closely into a company's production system. Beyond these standard indicators, there are indicators that address some of the unique issues that require attention and measurement when purchasing from underserved communities.

The first issue is how well the company is doing in developing profitable purchasing relationships with vendors from underserved markets. To measure this, companies track purchases from these vendors and gather information on vendor issues and concerns by line of business. Is the company doing a good job of identifying excellent vendors and integrating them into its supply chain? What issues need management attention?

Second, companies track how well the vendors from these markets are improving their competency and capacity. They track whether their suppliers are developing the appropriate certifications and meeting internal quality standards. They also track indicators of their suppliers' financial health and stability.

Finally, companies try to capture the ways in which purchasing from these suppliers improves creativity and product development. To do this, companies often gather anecdotal evidence from operations, sales, and R&D regarding the ways that having a diverse supplier group is helping to achieve goals. They promote stories and examples on best practices in these areas. They also share access to the best vendors across groups in the company.

PUTTING IT ALL TOGETHER: CASE STUDY

Green Mountain Coffee, Inc., has successfully engaged with underserved communities to create value through its supply chain. Green Mountain Coffee is a leader in the specialty coffee industry and has been recognized by *Forbes* magazine for the past three years (2002–2004) as one of the "200 Best Small Companies in America." The Company roasts high-quality arabica coffees and offers over 75 coffee selections including single-origins, estates, certified organics, Fair Trade, proprietary blends, and flavored coffees that it sells under the Green Mountain Coffee Roasters (GMCR) brand. The majority of GMCR's revenue is derived from its wholesale operation that serves supermarkets, convenience stores, offices, and other locations. The company achieved sales of $137 million for FY 2004.

Although stories usually start at the beginning, we'd like to start this one at the end. The punch line of the story is that Green Mountain was able to build sales and profits by adding certified Fair Trade coffee to its line of coffees. The Fair Trade and Organic certified line is GMCR's fastest-growing product line, accounting for approximately 16 percent of GMCR's sales in FY 2004. It has grown very rapidly—from 11 percent in FY 2003 to 16 percent in FY 2004. And in 2005, GMCR announced its goal of having 35 percent of its coffee sales be Fair Trade and Organic certified by the end of FY 2008.

These results are dramatic. But the process of reaching these results required a lot of hard work and some calculated risk-taking. During the process, Green Mountain used all five of the success factors to achieve these results.

Green Mountain is both a publicly traded company and a company with a deep commitment to environmental and social responsibility. As a publicly traded company, it faces the same pressures for quarterly earnings growth and solid financial results that all its peers face. As a company with a deep commitment to environmental and social responsibility, it faces the daily challenge of "walking the talk." Each day, it has to both stay true to its values and also make the profits that its investors require.

■ 1. MINE AND TRANSLATE LOCAL MARKET INFORMATION

Before Fair Trade certification even came into view, GMCR executives had had regular and deep contact with individuals in underserved communities, since essentially all the coffee it buys is grown in underserved communities. These contacts derived from (1) regular business visits to farms to evaluate farm management and review coffee quality, and (2) the engagement of the company and staff with nonprofit organizations such as Coffee Kids, a nonprofit that seeks to improve the quality of life for children and families who live in coffee-growing communities. From this personal experience, some Green Mountain Coffee executives saw that there was a potential win-win relationship among coffee quality, coffee price, and a better standard of living for the coffee growers.

Bob Stiller, the CEO of Green Mountain, felt that Fair Trade certification offered the key to unlocking both a better price for farmers and increased sales for the company. Certification provides critically important information to both the company and the consumer, ensuring that the coffee really is purchased on terms that benefit the farmers, and that the monetary benefits really do flow through to the individual growers. He looked to TransFair USA, an independent third-party certifier of Fair Trade in the United States, to provide this critical information.

■ 2. ADAPT BUSINESS MODEL TO COMMMUNITY REALITIES

While TransFair's certification was useful, it came at a cost and would require some changes in Green Mountain Coffee's business model. The first, and biggest, change was paying more for coffee. TransFair required that Green Mountain Coffee pay a "fair price." This price was set on an international basis at a level that would allow small coffee farmers to make a decent living. For example, in 2004, the "fair price" for coffee was $1.26 per pound. But this was in some cases 75 percent to 100 percent of the prevailing international price at that time. The second change was that Green Mountain Coffee would have to pay an extra 10 cents per pound licensing fee to TransFair for its certification services. As Green Mountain Coffee struggled to decide whether and how to launch its Fair Trade line, there were many heated discussions among the company's staff. Would it sell? Would it ever be profitable? If only some of Green Mountain Coffee's lines were certified as "Fair Trade," wouldn't that imply that the rest were "UnFair Trade"? These and many other issues were not easy to resolve.

■ 3. CHANGE INTERNAL INCENTIVES AND CHALLENGE CULTURAL ASSUMPTIONS

Bob Stiller, the CEO, was the champion for this product. He wanted the company to have a Fair Trade line, and he wanted the managers to figure out how to do it. Keeping the CEO happy was the critical internal incentive that supplied the energy to move forward the process of developing the product line.

Even though the CEO wanted to have a Fair Trade line, internal challenges were raised about how to do so profitably; these took eight months to resolve. In order to launch the line, Green Mountain had to think about how to package and promote the product to its own sales force, and how to educate employees, customers, and ultimately individual coffee-drinkers about why Fair Trade mattered and why the Green Mountain Coffee line was worth the extra cost. One of the most significant challenges came from the sales force, which viewed Fair Trade coffee as just another coffee flavor, rather than seeing it as a way to open up new markets.

The CEO established an internal team to manage the product development process. The team used success stories and anecdotes supplied by TransFair and others to show that there was a market for the product and that it could help increase sales. Whenever there was a meeting, they put this topic on the agenda. Eventually, the decision was made to launch the line by focusing on accounts in which there was likely to be a very high customer interest in the Fair

Trade label, and to start with a limited number of products. The coffee did cost somewhat more than other brands, but it was of consistently high quality and was clearly more socially responsible. The key was finding channels (such as organic and whole food stores, and university food services) where the customer demand would drive the acceptance of the product, and where there was a lower degree of price sensitivity.

■ 4. CREATE PARTNERSHIPS AND STRATEGIC ALLIANCES

Green Mountain Coffee has created a mutually beneficial partnership with TransFair that has been a critical part of achieving success. TransFair certifies the coffee as meeting Fair Trade standards, which helps create customer confidence that the product is truly socially responsible. Equally important, TransFair builds demand for Fair Trade coffee among consumers and retailers. It does this through a concentrated program of public relations and community organizing. TransFair actively partners with environmental, faith-based, student, and consumer organizations to generate grassroots consumer demand and promotional support for Fair Trade products on a national level. For example, when Fair Trade was launched in the United States in September 2000, TransFair worked with Oxfam America to create a postcard campaign requesting Fair Trade coffee at all the universities where there were Oxfam chapters. This helped move several universities, including Columbia University, to put a Fair Trade coffee into their coffee line-up. Similarly, TransFair has worked with the National Association of College and University Food Services to promote Fair Trade in this segment.

TransFair has continued to invest in market-building activities for Fair Trade products and has been successful in generating media interest and coverage. For example, more than 40 articles per month were published about Fair Trade in 2004, in publications—including *Time*, the *New York Times*, the *Wall Street Journal*, and dozens of leading food-and-beverage-industry trade publications—that reached a combined readership of more than 98 million people across North America. TransFair's success in generating increased customer demand has led to benefits both for Green Mountain Coffee and for coffee growers.

■ 5. IMPROVE THE ENABLING ENVIRONMENT

Through its work with TransFair, and also directly through its own philanthropic activities, Green Mountain is helping to improve the enabling environment in the communities where the coffee is grown. Producer cooperatives are being established to provide technical assistance, credit, and market information to coffee growers. Farmers reinvest a portion of Fair Trade revenues in community services such as health clinics, schools, scholarship programs, better housing, and women's programs. Health and education programs are today being implemented by more than 80 percent of the cooperatives selling to the U.S. market. These activities help to create more stable communities, a better workforce, and in the long run a more sustainable source of high-quality coffee. This is a win-win relationship for business and community alike.

■ CONCLUSION ■

Companies can improve sales and reduce risks to brands by increasing purchasing from underserved communities in ways that create a win-win relationship for both sides. It's not always easy. In many cases, creating a mutually beneficial purchasing relationship with vendors from underserved communities requires purchasing staff to invest more time than with other vendors and sometimes pay a higher price per unit. This investment makes business sense only when there is a clear benefit to sales or a clear reduction of risks to brand and reputation.

The business benefit can be traced to consumer expectations. If consumers care enough to buy a brand that has a win-win purchasing relationship with underserved communities—or to penalize brands that are perceived as unfairly exploiting workers in underserved communities—there can be a clear business benefit to investing the necessary time and energy. If not, building such purchasing relationships may be worth doing on moral grounds, but companies shouldn't expect to sell more product in the process.

Implementing this type of purchasing strategy may require the company to work with brokering and certification organizations to help it find the right suppliers and ensure that these suppliers will create benefits for brand and reputation. It also can involve helping to build supplier capacity by transferring skills from purchaser to supplier.

Because this type of purchasing benefits a number of departments across the company, including sales, brand management, and community relations, it is important to create cross-departmental teams to implement the strategy. Support from top management is crucial.

Purchasing from underserved communities in ways that are mutually beneficial enables your company to position purchasing as a strategic asset. With this strategy, purchasing not only provides needed supplies in a timely way at the best price, but also helps build your company's sales, brand, and reputation. This type of purchasing strategy also helps businesses in underserved communities to thrive, creating jobs and income, even wealth, for residents.

For additional case studies and further details, see the following websites:

Codes of Conduct: www.codesofconduct.org
Institute for Supply Management: www.ism.ws
International Business Leaders Forum: www.iblf.org
National Minority Supplier Development Corporation: www.nmsdcus.org
Social Accountability International: www.sa-intl.org
TransFair USA: www.transfairusa.org
Win-Win Partners: www.winwinpartner.com

4

ACCELERATING PRODUCT AND PROCESS INNOVATION

Are you feeling an increasing pressure to accelerate the pace of product and process innovation? Have you ever felt tempted to proclaim, as did a sign posted in the office of an R&D manager, "The necessity of invention is a mother!"? If so, this chapter will be welcome, because it will provide you with insights into how engaging with underserved communities can accelerate and expand your company's ability to produce commercially rewarding product and process innovations.

But can engaging with underserved markets really make a difference? Why should engaging with communities that have fewer resources than mainstream communities, that may have cultural or language barriers, and that may be geographically or politically isolated actually help to accelerate innovation? While this may seem counter-intuitive, it is supported both by theory and experience. Innovation is not spurred by an abundance of resources. Rather, it is spurred by novelty and by need. Innovation, particularly radical innovation, requires breaking out of standard patterns of thinking and organization. Engaging in a profound way with communities that are very different from mainstream communities can provide the stimulation needed to shake up preconceptions and challenge standard thought patterns.

Innovation is also spurred by pressing needs or extreme technical demands. Think of the ingenious innovations created by people who are shipwrecked or stranded in the wilderness. The need to stay alive under adverse circumstances with very limited resources catalyzes creative thought and solutions that would never come to mind in less demanding situations. The residents of underserved communities have faced very demanding situations as well and they've developed innovative ways to address their challenges. Their experience can be mined for innovative approaches that can be useful for serving those markets and sometimes for other contexts as well.

The development of the Internet is an example of how extreme technical challenges can lead to unexpected innovative breakthroughs. Consider that the precursor to the Internet—DARPANet—was developed to meet an extreme technical challenge: the need for a communications network that would continue to function effectively even if part of the network was destroyed by a nuclear strike. That extreme technical requirement led to the fundamental architecture of the Internet—the breaking of all communication into tiny discrete packets of information, all of which had data describing the sender and the recipient, which enabled that information to be sent along different pathways at different times and yet still get from sender to receiver. This architecture is partly responsible for the Internet's tremendous growth and flexibility. These features also would never have emerged from systems developed under much more resource-rich conditions— as telephone service demonstrates.

This chapter focuses primarily on process and product innovations that will help your company increase sales and profits in underserved markets. This is the type of innovation that is most directly accelerated by increased interaction with underserved markets. But there are many examples of innovations that were developed for underserved markets and then turned out to help sales in mainstream markets as well. For example, the Fannie Mae innovation in mortgage products profiled in Chapter 1 was developed to meet the specific requirement of low-wealth, low-income, first-time homebuyers. But the mortgage product—a low-downpayment product that didn't require three years of employment at the same job—turned out to be very attractive to young, first-time homebuyers from mainstream communities who weren't able to amass the 20 percent down required by more traditional mortgage products. The low-downpayment products are now offered by many financial institutions in many markets.

To get the innovation benefits of engagement with underserved markets, you most likely will have to change the way your company generates ideas for innovation and the way it sorts through and chooses among those ideas for product and process development. You must get the managers involved in the innovation process to obtain more information from underserved communities and to test out ideas coming from these markets.

UNDERSTANDING THE INCREASING PRESSURE FOR INNOVATION

Innovation is seen to be a critical factor in sustaining and strengthening the competitiveness of companies. A recent Bain & Company survey of global senior executives (across all sectors) found that 86 percent believed that "innovation is more important than cost reduction for long-term success." Similarly, the World Economic Forum, the world's leading business organization, places considerable emphasis on innovation as a means of increasing national productivity. Put simply: the more companies are able to derive value from unique products and processes, the stronger their basis of competitive advantage (Rigby and Bilodeau, 2005; Cornelius, Schwab, and Porter, 2003).

Innovation is important, and the pace of innovation is accelerating. According to a survey of 188 global companies completed in 2004 by *The Economist,* at least 25 percent of their revenue derived from products and services less than three years old (George, Works, and Watson-Hemphill, 2005). This continuous need for new products and services provides intense pressure on innovation to accelerate.

In the context of this book, we have taken "innovation" to mean both product and process innovations. The following factors are making both types of innovation an important strategic imperative today and increasing the need for an accelerated rate of innovation:

- *Globalization.* With increased global competition, to be successful firms must continually produce innovations to maintain their market power, which competition continually erodes. In Chapter 1, we discussed opportunities to reach untapped markets through what Christensen and Hart refer to as "disruptive innovations." Disruptive innovations "either create new markets or reshape existing markets by delivering relatively simple, convenient, low-cost innovations to a set of customers who are ignored by industry leaders" (Hart and Christensen, 2002).

- *Technological change.* The speed of technological change and the extent to which new products and services can alter market conditions mean that the challenge to innovate is continuous. As mentioned in earlier chapters, the innovative application of technology can be leveraged by companies to reach untapped niches in underserved markets in a more cost-efficient way.

- *Consumer revolution.* The average consumer in developed countries—well educated, empowered by the Internet, with easy access to credit, and informed by 24/7 media—is exerting personal values in purchasing decisions, causing companies to re-engineer critical aspects of production in order to be more social and environmentally responsible. The Eco-imagination initiative of General Electric, announced in 2005, is a good example of this trend. This initiative reflects GE's belief that future company growth will benefit from developing innovative, environmentally friendly technologies that avoid fossil fuels, increase energy efficiency, and reduce greenhouse gas emissions.

- *Economic liberalization.* The combination of deregulation and privatization over the last 30 years around the globe has contributed vastly to spurring innovation across multiple industry sectors—from telecommunications to financial services and utilities.

- *Geopolitics.* The global reliance on oil from the Middle East is contributing to the development of alternative fuels, affecting not only natural resource companies but all industrial users of energy (e.g., the transportation industry). The unpredictability of global terrorism will also require industry to consider keeping infrastructure investments geographically diverse, placing a premium on being a good corporate citizen in order to protect one's license to operate. Companies that create innovative approaches to solving social problems in developing countries will be better able to protect their license to operate.

Given these strategic imperatives, how can your company employ the five success factors to achieve innovation in underserved markets?

ACCELERATING PRODUCT AND PROCESS INNOVATION

Your company probably has a well-developed approach to product and process innovation. It has ways for gathering information about customer interests and needs, about potential innovations, and about likely moves by competitors in creating new products and services. It has methods for sifting through the potential innovations and choosing those that will be developed and market-tested. And the managers of the innovation process most likely have keen intuitions about where potentially profitable innovation lies, and they have used these intuitions to guide the process well over time. If they didn't, they probably wouldn't still be managers of the process.

So why does any of this need to change? Because all of this, most likely, is based on mainstream markets. And this approach won't be as effective in generating profitable innovations in products and processes for underserved markets as it is for mainstream markets. To develop innovations for underserved markets, it is critical to change the innovation and development process within your company so that it can capture information and ideas from the interactions that your company has with consumers and thought leaders in those underserved markets. The effort to change can lead to innovations suited for these markets and also, on occasion, for mainstream markets as well.

■ I. MINE AND TRANSLATE LOCAL INFORMATION

What's Different about Underserved Markets

The best source of information and ideas for products that can meet the needs of customers in underserved markets are the residents of those markets themselves. This is not surprising; after all, to design products that customers want, companies typically talk to the customers first and then design the products. The problem is that many businesses based in mainstream markets don't have the kinds of pro-

> **What's different?**
>
> - Businesses don't have processes in place to gather useful information from underserved markets to spur innovation.
>
> **What to do about it.**
>
> - Re-engineer community engagement processes to develop information that's useful for innovation.
> - Engage in collaborative efforts to lower costs of generating valuable information.

cesses in place that let them gather information that helps to generate profitable innovations in underserved markets.

What to Do in Underserved Markets

In order to understand the kind of information that is needed, we have to glance forward to the next success factor—adapting the business model. The information that your company needs to collect depends on the kinds of adaptation to its products and processes that it needs to make. For simplicity's sake, we can characterize innovation as being one of two types: incremental innovation, or strategic innovation. Incremental innovation involves making improvements on an existing product or process. Companies sometimes refer to this as "localizing" a product—slightly adjusting its features and design so that it better fits the local market needs and environment. This does not require a deep understanding of the market, and it can often be done with the help of local marketing and advertising firms.

Strategic innovation is much more difficult to do from a distance. This type of innovation involves creating entirely new products or technologies and then deploying them in novel and unexpected ways. When successful, it can open an entirely new market. The development of the iPod and iTunes provides a good example outside the context of underserved markets. The iPod and iTunes entirely changed the paradigm for distributing and selling music over the Internet. It also created a hugely profitable market advantage for Apple, which controls roughly 75 percent of the market for downloaded music sales today.

Strategic innovation requires being steeped in the world of the consumer or user of the product. It often requires making unexpected connections or seeing "out of the box" opportunities or possibilities. The innovation manager has to have accurate intuitions about what customers want and will pay for, so that he or she can guide a radically new product to a successful launch. All of this is much more achievable if the manager has accurate and in-depth information about the markets.

How do companies get this information when most of their staff are based in communities that are mainstream, rather than underserved? There are two key strategies:

1. *Re-engineer community engagement to generate information useful for innovation.* Companies often have some form of engagement with underserved communities—as customers, employees, or sites for volunteer work. These engagements can be redirected and rechanneled to provide information on customer needs and behaviors that can be used to spark innovation.

2. *Engage in collaborations to lower the cost of gaining information.* Gathering and analyzing in-depth information on a wide variety of potential market niches in underserved communities can be expensive. As noted in Chapter 1, these markets typically don't have information that is as complete and as accurate as do markets that are well served. The economy of scale that drives down the cost of information about well-served markets doesn't exist in underserved markets. Companies can create that scale by collaborating to explore potential markets for innovative products and services.

Re-engineer Engagement with Communities

Your company probably engages with individuals in underserved communities in many ways. It may sell products or services to them, or sell to companies that sell to them. It may hire them as employees. They may be part of the company's supply chain. Some employees may volunteer in these communities, or your company may provide grants to organizations working in these communities. But odds are good that none of these engagements are structured so that they produce information that feeds into your company's innovation process.

You are missing an opportunity. You can re-engineer these engagements so that they do generate information that feeds into the innovation processes. You can mine the information that is already available to your company to spark innovative ideas and approaches. You may even be able to redeploy some of the individuals who are engaging with these communities in a way that is more useful for innovation.

In the mid-1990s, CEMEX, the world's second-largest cement maker and one of Mexico's largest companies, dramatically re-engineered its engagement with underserved communities in order to develop a strategic innovation. This innovation sprang from the significant reduction in its sales caused by Mexico's crippling currency devaluation. The new form of engagement enabled the company to create the Patrimonio Hoy product line, which led to dramatically increased sales for the company and better housing for community residents.

In its search for increased sales, the company decided to pursue the do-it-yourself homebuilding market, which is the most common form of homebuilding in lower-income Mexican neighborhoods. The individuals who built their own homes had long used CEMEX's cement, but typically had bought from middlemen rather than CEMEX directly. However, the information coming back to CEMEX from this distribution channel didn't tell it how to successfully innovate to serve this market.

CEMEX needed to dramatically change the way that it engaged with these communities to generate information for innovation. To this end, a team of ten professionals lived in different low-income neighborhoods for a year, gathering in-depth information on how people made money, how they purchased materials and built in one-room increments, and how they pooled money to finance their purchases. Their detailed observations enabled CEMEX to create the Patrimonio Hoy program.

The Patrimonio Hoy program was a significant innovation to CEMEX's existing sales approach. Instead of selling just building materials, it combined financing, architectural advice, and building materials into one package. It also focused on long-term customer relationships rather than single-sales opportunities. The design of the program was based on *tandas*, a common form of savings group in

Mexico. In a typical *tanda,* every member contributes 100 pesos each week, and each week a different member receives the entire group sum until each has taken the pool once. CEMEX created Patrimonio Hoy clubs, similar to *tandas,* into which each member contributed a small amount of money each week. Instead of receiving a pot of money, group members received the materials to build their next room. They also received architectural and technical advice about which building materials were right for the rooms they wanted to build, as well as warehousing and delivery services. The business model for this program was built through successive pilots, each increasing in scale.

CEMEX used an external organization to conduct an evaluation of the experience of the first 1,000 families in the program. The results were dramatic. Prior to Patrimonio Hoy, typical customers built an average of one room every four to seven years. In contrast, members of CEMEX's *tanda* clubs built an average of one room every 1.5 years. Equally important from a family perspective, the construction waste was significantly reduced because the correct amount of materials for building the room arrived when needed and there was no waste due to deterioration during on-site storage. In addition to increasing the pace of building, the number of families building additions grew and the average amount that the family was able to save from earnings and spend on building increased from $240 to almost $600. This was a win both for the families and for CEMEX. The families were able to build more rooms for their homes—two to three more rooms than they originally had planned—and CEMEX sold more cement faster than it had before.

Based on this positive evaluation of the program success, CEMEX was able to expand the program quickly, and it had 70,000 Mexican families enrolled in the program as of 2005. CEMEX is planning to expand the program to other countries as well (CEMEX, 2005; Sandoval, 2005; Vision, 2005).

The CEMEX approach to re-engineering engagement with the community involves a deep immersion of the innovation team in the community, so that they can (1) study the way community members manage their lives, and (2) better understand both the challenges community residents experience in meeting their needs and how the company can provide products and services to help them meet those challenges.

Another approach is to leverage the knowledge of your company's vendors or distributors—people already doing business in the community who are also from the community. The partnership noted in Chapter 3 between Kroger and Glory Foods to develop a new line of frozen dinners provides a good example. The management of Glory Foods had considerable experience in selling into underserved communities, and many managers themselves were drawn from underserved communities. Their firsthand experience of the prospective customers' likes and dislikes helped shape successful innovation in merchandising and distribution.

A third approach is to use employee volunteerism as a means of acquiring new knowledge and skills to generate innovation. When managers get involved in communities as volunteers, they can learn in more depth about customer needs and interests, which can then shed light on innovation in product and process. For example, managers and staff at Travelers Property Casualty have a long tradition of volunteer service to residents of underserved communities, which helped shape the development of the Loss Prevention Partnership noted in Chapter 1.

Join Business Collaborations That Identify Innovation Opportunities

When businesses conduct their initial explorations into potential new markets, they often join a collaborative effort as a way of leveraging existing knowledge, reducing research time, and lowering the cost of acquiring useful information. Several such collaboratives have been created recently to explore innovation opportunities in underserved markets. One example is the Sustainable Livelihoods Project at the World Business Council for Sustainable Development. This project is chaired by executives from BP, GrupoNueva, and Eskom. The goal of the project is to build inclusive business models that create new revenue streams while serving the needs of the poor through profitable commercial operations.

The Sustainable Livelihoods Project creates a shared space for learning and sharing, as well as shared costs for research and analysis. The participating companies have provided case studies from their own operations of both successes and challenges in selling to, hiring from, and purchasing from underserved communities. The companies pay for a shared research staff that gathers additional information, maintains a joint Web site, and develops field guides and "how to" tip sheets. Managers from the participating businesses also have formed learning groups, organized by region or industry, to meet for off-the-record discussions about their challenges, strategies, and progress. Since its formation in 2003, the project has produced four field guides for its members and many case studies of specific business approaches. These include the provision of financial services, energy, water, housing, and information and communication technology to underserved markets (World Business Council for Sustainable Development, 2005).

A second example is the Base of the Pyramid Protocol Project. This two-year project, started in 2004, seeks to generate insight into the processes by which firms can identify and develop sustainable new products and business models in partnership with underserved, very low income communities. To that end, the project will establish and test a "protocol" (a detailed working methodology) for under-

---

Management Tips: "Base of the Pyramid" Operating Guidelines

Guidelines for business success developed by the Base of the Pyramid Protocol Project:

- *Suspend disbelief*—willingness to admit ignorance
- *Put the last first*—seek out voices seldom heard
- *Show respect and humility*—all parties have something important to contribute
- *Accept and respect divergent views*—there is no best way
- *Recognize the positive*—people who survive on $1 per day must be doing something right
- *Co-develop solutions*—mutual learning among multinational corporations, partners, and BoP members
- *Create mutual value*—all parties must benefit in terms important to them
- *Start small*—begin with small pilot tests, and scale out in modular fashion
- *Be patient*—it takes time to grow the [market system] and win the trust before business takes off

Source: Simanis et al., 2005.

standing the needs, perspectives, and capabilities of these communities and meeting them in a way that provides value to the communities and the corporations.

The key project outcomes include (1) a robust research protocol that will facilitate a range of companies' efforts to develop knowledge and capabilities necessary for serving BoP markets and consumers, (2) an understanding of how to engage in the design of sustainable business models together with communities that meet the needs of present and future generations of community residents, and (3) insight into the design and marketing of sustainable products and services in these communities. The project partners are drawn from businesses (SC Johnson, DuPont, and Hewlett-Packard) and management schools (Cornell, UNC Chapel Hill, and University of Michigan) (Base of the Pyramid Protocol Project, 2005). See the box on page 141 for more tips from the Base of the Pyramid Protocol Project.

■ 2. ADAPT BUSINESS MODEL TO COMMUNITY REALITIES

What's Different about Underserved Markets

What's different?

- Locating community engagement solely within community relations function isolates information that's valuable for innovation.

What to do about it.

- Engage line managers in projects in underserved communities.
- Develop partnerships between business units and community relations units.
- Partner with or purchase companies that are successful innovators in these markets.

If your company does not already have a significant business line selling to underserved markets, and doesn't have a significant employment base in an underserved community, it's likely that the only part of your company that has regular engagement with underserved communities is the community relations department. And if your company is like most other companies, the community relations department has no connection to the departments charged with innovation and product development. They simply don't communicate on a regular basis.

That's fine if you are not trying to innovate in ways that depend on insights into underserved markets.

But it's a problem if you have to develop products and services for these markets, or if you want to gain insights from these markets to improve services and products for mainstream markets.

What to Do in Underserved Markets

There are three ways to change the business model and increase innovation for underserved markets. The first is to engage line managers in the projects in the community, so that they can get a first-hand look at opportunities and barriers to innovation. The managers may be drawn from different parts of the company in different industries. For example, in the high-tech industry, the managers that are most important to get involved are from the R&D labs. In insurance and banking, it's the executives in line management positions that are most important. In other industries, it may be the sales force managers. The point is to get the managers responsible for product and service innovation into direct contact with the community for which innovation needs to occur.

The second approach is to develop partnerships between business units and community relations units. These partnerships can be structured so that both units have specific goals and roles and can gain benefits from their partnership. The partnerships can help business units to better understand opportunities for innovation in communities, while helping the community relations units build a more positive impact for the underserved community.

The third approach is to partner with or to purchase companies that are already successful innovators in these markets and to use their operating methods to spur innovations in your own company. These companies have already done the hard work of figuring out how to innovate successfully. The lessons they have learned can serve as a useful guide to your managers, pointing them toward productive areas for innovation and steering them clear of dead-ends or other difficulties.

Engage Line Managers

St. Paul Travelers provides insurance for home, auto, and business. Since 1994, one of its key community engagement activities has been its commitment to the National Insurance Task Force (NITF).

The NITF is a coalition of insurers, educational institutions, regulators, community-based organizations, and national nonprofits. Its mission is "to develop partnerships between the insurance industry and community-based organizations to better market the products and services of both, for the benefit of the customers and communities they serve."

The NITF is focused on improving the quality and affordability of homeowners insurance in low-income urban areas. One of the most important programs of the NITF is the Loss Prevention Partnership (LPP) program, noted previously in Chapter 1. The LPP program involves nonprofits, insurers, and city agencies working to identify and remediate the causes of homeowners' loss in low-income neighborhoods. The LPP program had pilot sites in six cities across the United States and received $4.5 million in grant funding and $2.5 million in low-interest, long-term loans from St. Paul Travelers, other insurers, and foundations. Each site had a sponsoring community-based organization and a coordinating committee comprised of local insurers, nonprofits, banks, and city agencies.

The committee and the sponsoring organization designed the remediation activities, and the sponsoring organization implemented them. For example, the pilot site in Chicago was focused on addressing the peril of fire. Homeowners learned to understand how faulty heating, wiring, and appliances can lead to hazardous situations. The home safety evaluation focused closely on the home's heating, electrical, and cooking appliances. The program also made low-interest, long-term loans that helped homeowners to repair or replace boilers, furnaces, wiring, and the like.

Many companies might have assigned the task of working with NITF to a community relations professional. Instead, St. Paul Travelers made a significant commitment of the time of its senior executives to the work of the NITF. St. Paul Travelers has had five representatives serve on the NITF—Ed Charlebois, who is responsible for all home insurance in the United States; Don Davis, who is responsible for increasing urban market sales across the United States; Bill Allen and Jeff Graham, who report to Davis; and Bill Lawrence, Davis's counterpart in Travelers Commercial Lines. Charlebois served as the NITF chairperson for two years.

This deep engagement by business executives to the NITF project was unusual, and it led to some unusual results. In particular, their hands-on experience with the customers and remediation efforts in underserved markets gave them important insights into these markets. These insights helped them create process innovations in the units they managed, developing improvements for products sold both in underserved markets and in mainstream markets. For example, they were able to improve and clarify underwriting guidelines, which are critical to sustained profitability. They also were able to successfully resolve regulatory issues in a number of states—issues that would have affected sales in both the underserved and mainstream markets across those states. In addition, they found ways of improving customer service, which is key to retention and long-term profits (Sabapathy et al., 2003; Weiser and Zadek, 2000).

Develop Partnerships Between Innovation Units and Community Engagement

By developing internal partnerships between innovation units and community engagement units, companies can create innovations that are valuable for both the company and the community. The process that IBM developed for creating partnerships between its Corporate Community Relations department (CCR) and a number of its research labs provides a good example. The research labs are the units of the company charged with developing research and innovations that enable the company to address immediate needs as well as future opportunities. IBM has designated specific individuals with the responsibility of linking the research labs to other business units, and it has provided budgeting support for the linkages. Through this process, a number of the research labs have worked closely with CCR and external stakeholders on pressing social problems that present new technical product challenges. The project work solves social problems and also generates innovative products and services, both for underserved communities and for major markets as well. According to Stanley S. Litow, vice president of corporate community relations for IBM,

> IBM's corporate citizenship activities used to be separate from its business functions. Now IBM's research centers innovate for the business and the researchers work closely with community

groups and public agencies to develop products and services that address education and social needs. These products have many commercial applications that support our shift from being a hardware company into a services and solutions company, but the point is to address community needs as our first priority. (Sabapathy et al., 2003)

This approach to product innovation is illustrated here by the development of IBM's "transcoding" technology, an Internet-based technology that allows users to change the way Web pages are displayed so that they are easier to read, understand, and interact with. Transcoding represented a significant advance from existing technologies and markedly increased the ability of individuals with sensory impairments to use Web pages and access the Internet. At the time that this technology was in development, the technical challenges were so significant that some IBM managers doubted whether it could be viably developed.

The research labs contacted the CCR team because the liaison between research labs and CCR saw that CCR could help research labs connect to community networks that would provide insight and information useful in the development of transcoding. The CCR team in turn recognized the significant benefits that transcoding could offer for an underserved market—in this case, people with disabilities. CCR and the research labs chose to develop the transcoding technology together with SeniorNet, a nonprofit with which IBM had a long-standing relationship. SeniorNet's senior citizen clientele often have multiple disabilities, including impaired vision, reduced motor dexterity, and limited hearing—impairments that the transcoding project was designed to address.

SeniorNet worked closely with the team from CCR and the research labs in coordinating the development, testing, and refining of the transcoding software. SeniorNet identified stakeholders who were interested in using the technology and training others to use it. SeniorNet helped IBM to understand how the users were interacting with the product and to develop better interfaces and help menus. SeniorNet created a database to track problems and a help desk for its users, staffed by people who understand both its users and the transcoding product. It also was able to place all of the program documentation on line, so users could resolve some of their own questions without the need for additional help. This helped SeniorNet's staff to give IBM detailed information on the nature of the problems that were occurring and the likely changes required to fix them.

The partnership helped the research labs to successfully develop the technology, which has been incorporated into a range of IBM products and services, including Web-hosting services and support for Internet Service Providers. The market for "disability friendly" products and services is significant and growing. Beyond the immediate value to IBM's business and to Web users with various sensory impairments, the development of transcoding technology has allowed IBM to strengthen its position ahead of U.S. regulations that require the federal government to provide equal access to information on Web sites for all employees and citizens, including disabled individuals. The successful development of the transcoding technology was also a significant benefit to the seniors whom SeniorNet served, as it made it much easier for them to access the Web and interact with Web content. All these outcomes derived from IBM's internal process of creating a partnership between the research labs and the Corporate Community Relations department, which provided the glue that connected the labs, CCR, and SeniorNet (Sabapathy et al., 2003).

Partner With or Purchase Successful Innovators in These Markets

The underserved markets that you are targeting may not have many major corporations serving them, but they do typically have a vibrant set of smaller companies that provide products and services. These smaller companies have learned through firsthand experience how to sell profitably into these markets and how to create innovations in product and process to meet the demands of consumers in these markets. If you can find a company that is selling products or services that complement the ones you are seeking to develop, it can help to drive innovation in your company.

The strongest potential partners or acquisitions in these markets are companies whose innovations can be integrated well into your current strategy. One important criterion for choosing a partner or acquisition is that its innovations be scalable and transferable. You want to be able to take innovations developed in one underserved community and bring them to many others in a cost-effective way across the globe. Innovations that depend on unique local circumstances, or that can't be increased much in volume, are much less attractive than those capable of being scaled up. Second, the innovation should enable consumers to purchase a range of products from your existing product line. The more that the innovation can help cross-selling to these new customers, the more support you will be able to garner for the sometimes challenging process of entering the market and implementing the innovation. Finally, it is very helpful if the innovation is data-driven. The more that the innovation is supported by clear data about the market and the consumers, the easier it will be to persuade other managers within your company to adopt the innovation and integrate it into their own approaches.

The partnership between Union Bank and Nix Check Cashers is an interesting example. Union Bank was seeking to expand its provision of financial services to underserved markets in the United States. Initially, Union Bank entered the markets on its own. It started by creating a Cash and Save program, which included check-cashing as well as more traditional banking services. The program was targeted at low-income individuals and piloted in 13 bank branches and retail settings in California.

The results from this innovation were not as positive as had been hoped. The check-cashing services located in the Union Bank branches did not attract the planned volume of customers. But then a chance to invest in Nix Check Cashers provided the opportunity to take advantage of the experience of a company that already had successfully innovated in these markets. In 2000, Union Bank bought a partial ownership interest in Nix Check Cashers. The two companies also established a partnership with Operation Hope, a nonprofit specializing in financial education for low-income consumers. Together, the three organizations were able to successfully develop an innovative range of product offerings that were attractive to low-income consumers. These products included check cashing, savings, financial education, and ATM facilities, all geared to work together to meet the needs and interests of these consumers. By

2003, 31 joint facilities had been opened, and thousands of profitable new customers had been added by the partnership. Consumers in underserved communities benefited because they were getting access to a much broader array of financial services and paying less for most of them as well. Union Bank is in the process of expanding the innovation to other sites across its network.

This partnership exemplifies all three criteria noted above. First, the innovation was scalable. Check cashing is an almost universal need across underserved communities in the United States, and Nix Check Cashers' approach could be scaled up with technology familiar to Union Bank. Second, the innovation allowed cross-selling. It was not focused solely on check cashing but included savings, ATMs, and other financial services. The provision of financial education by the nonprofit Operation Hope was important in the cross-selling; the financial education helped consumers from these markets to understand the importance, and benefits, of establishing a savings account. Finally, the partners developed clear data about market demand and product profitability, which helped address skepticism both within Nix (which was concerned about losing check-cashing customers as they became savings-account customers at Union Bank) and within Union Bank (which was concerned that the savings-account customers would not be profitable). The data showed clearly that the joint approach led to profits for both sides of the partnership (Center for Corporate Citizenship, 2004).

■ 3. CHANGE INTERNAL INCENTIVES AND CHALLENGE CULTURAL ASSUMPTIONS

What's Different about Underserved Markets

In most companies, there is a limited and precious pot of resources that can be used to support product research and development. There is a high level of competition for these resources. There are many more good ideas that beg for research and development than there are dollars to investigate them. To manage this competition, the company has guidelines, policies, and incentives that shape the way those resources are employed. Usually, guidelines focus the

> **What's different?**
>
> - Company culture and incentives keep innovation focus away from underserved markets.
>
> **What to do about it.**
>
> - Create explicit incentives for managers who drive innovation to engage with underserved communities.
> - Embed community perspectives into innovation teams.
> - Use governance, company codes, and external commitments to drive engagement across the company.

research and development dollars on products and services for mainstream markets, not underserved ones. In addition, individuals who are successful at managing innovation processes typically have a knack for intuiting which avenues of research and development are likely to be fruitful, and which are likely to be dead ends. If they don't have well-developed intuitions—a "nose" for good new ideas and approaches—they can waste a lot of money and time developing products that never make it to the market. But these managers usually don't have much firsthand experience with underserved markets, so their cultural experiences and intuitions often don't lead them to see how potential products and services for underserved markets might be winners and therefore deserve support in the research and development process.

What to Do in Underserved Markets

Companies that succeed in creating innovation for underserved communities create processes that engage the innovation manager in a dialogue with underserved communities, either directly, or through others in the company. This enables the innovation manager to improve his ability to predict the type of innovation that will be most attractive to individuals in underserved communities. Processes that the companies use include creating incentives for managers to engage with underserved communities, and ensuring that people who are part of the underserved community, or have extensive familiarity with the community, are part of the innovation team. Some companies also use company-wide structures or commitments, such as the governance structure, codes of conduct, or public commitments, to provide incentives for deeper engagement with underserved communities and more resources for innovations for products and services for those communities.

Create Incentives to Engage with Communities

The incentives that innovation units face usually encourage them to focus their time and attention in areas where product development will bring products to market quickly, profitably, and at significant volume. These incentives usually focus innovation attention on large, well-developed markets rather than underserved ones, which can be seen as lower margin, more complex, and lower volume. In order to get the innovation units to focus attention on these markets, it helps to create clear incentives for engaging with them and developing products and services focused on them.

The partnerships at IBM between the research labs and the CCR unit, noted above, are driven by just such a set of internal incentives. The key incentive derives from the company's budgeting system. Each research lab starts the year with roughly half of its budget funded from the general corporate account. The managers in the unit then have to find partners, inside or outside of the company, who are interested in the innovations that the research labs want to pursue and who are willing to provide a portion of the innovation project budget. This requirement creates a strong incentive for the research labs to engage in creative dialogue with the other units in the company about the most productive directions for research and development.

The CCR unit also has a budget, a significant portion of which comes in the form of IBM staff time and services. This budget can be used to support the research labs if CCR deems that to be an appropriate way to meet community needs. CCR's budget is limited, and it continually seeks to leverage IBM's strategic assets in its projects. For CCR to engage the research labs in developing products and services for underserved constituencies, it must feel that the research labs can dramatically increase the impact of the projects that it is supporting. This budgeting system establishes a dynamic that encourages the right conversations to take place between units engaged with underserved communities, and units engaged in innovation, so that areas for innovation are identified, pursued, and brought to these communities in a timely way.

Embed Community Perspectives

Companies can help spur innovation by embedding community perspectives into the groups that are charged with innovation. This can occur in a wide variety of ways. One approach is to hire talented and experienced people from the nonprofits and smaller businesses that are already serving the communities you are trying to reach. If you can hire smart, "street-wise" individuals and integrate them into the units charged with innovation in these markets, they can help transform internal opinions and assumptions about underserved communities and their market opportunities. These individuals' experience and relationships in the markets can help your managers connect to opportunities and ultimately create successful innovations. The U.S. banking industry provides a good example. Many top managers in the units that are developing new products and services for underserved communities were hired from community development finance organizations and other nonprofits providing financing in underserved markets. These managers have been responsible for the development of some of the most imaginative, and profitable, products and services created for this market.

Companies can also identify internal resources and bring them onto teams charged with innovation. Safeco, discussed in Chapter 1, used this approach when staffing its Diversity Marketing Committee. It sought to identify individuals within the firm who could bring personal experience and insight into these communities to the committee, to enable the committee to innovate more effectively.

A third approach is to work directly with community organizations to involve them in the product development process. The BBC's work in the Oxford Road community in the United Kingdom provides an example. Although the BBC is not a for-profit corporation, because it is a developer of radio programming that succeeds or fails based on audience interest, it faces many of the same challenges in developing innovative new programming as do for-profit corporations. BBC Berkshire, the local BBC station that serves the Reading area in the United Kingdom, was seeking a way to provide radio programming that would better engage listeners from the Oxford Road area of Reading—an underserved community. The area was notorious in the city for drugs, prostitution, and crime, but the BBC recognized it as a vibrant multicultural community. The positive community spirit in the area prompted the station to create a radio show to illustrate the good aspects of the community and debunk many of the stereotypes.

The Oxford Road Project asked residents to contribute stories of and ideas about life in their community. The BBC then created a 12-part radio drama using professional writers and actors. More than 500 local schoolchildren took part in the resulting drama workshops, and the series prompted new positive ties and celebrations within the Oxford Road community.

The model was innovative in that no local radio station had tried to develop a show using ideas from residents on this scale before. BBC Berkshire now knows it can turn to its often-overlooked local communities to find reliable programming material. The initiative also strengthened the station's local presence and has put the BBC at the center of the community (Business in the Community, 2005).

Use Governance, Company Codes, and External Commitments to Drive Engagement

Companies, particularly large, successful companies, often develop a momentum and a direction that are hard to redirect. But while this can lead to great success in core markets, it also can make it quite difficult to get managers to focus on new markets, particularly underserved ones. They can seem irrelevant.

Major changes in the company's environment, such as significant shifts in consumer demand, the source of future employees, or changing regulations, can provide the force that changes the direction of the company's momentum. The company needs to change the incentives for innovation, so that innovation occurs in ways that meet the new market or environmental demand.

Management can use a number of approaches to alter incentives on a company-wide basis. One approach is to change governance. For example, creating a committee of the board that is charged with overseeing engagement with a particular community can provide the impetus to drive change throughout the organization. Another approach is to incorporate the new direction or new level of engagement into a corporate code of conduct or a set of standard operating procedures. Much of the change and innovation in supply chain management has been driven through corporate codes of conduct. Finally, a company can use external commitments to help drive engagement. This can take many forms. For example, as part of its effort to increase minority purchasing, noted in Chapter 3, Texas Instruments (TI), made public commitments to workforce diversity and minority purchasing. TI reports on its progress against these commitments every year, and they are posted on its Web site. This effort provides steady incentive over time to keep the company engaged with underserved communities, and it helps propel innovation in purchasing and hiring.

▪ 4. CREATE PARTNERSHIPS AND STRATEGIC ALLIANCES

What's Different about Underserved Markets

Gaining information that is useful for innovation can be quite expensive. As noted in Chapter 1, information on underserved communities is often not as readily available as information on mainstream communities. Organizations that specialize in predicting market trends often don't focus on underserved consumers in the same detail as they do mainstream consumers. Underserved communities are often more difficult to survey, because they have less access to communications and because transportation can be more difficult. Members of underserved communities also may distrust survey takers and may feel that answering questions might open them up to scrutiny by government agencies.

It also can be expensive to bring innovation managers into day-to-day contact with these markets to get the kind of firsthand, in-depth information that guides the innovation process. Underserved communities are likely to be physically and culturally

---

What's different?

- Gaining information that is useful for innovation can be expensive and requires competencies beyond the core set of the business.

What to do about it.

- Look for potential win-win partnerships with organizations that collect information useful for innovation, or that can bring resources to help your company innovate successfully.

distant from the communities in which the innovation staff lives and works. As noted earlier in this chapter, in order to get the information needed to successfully develop Patrimonio Hoy, CEMEX had ten of its innovation staff live in the underserved communities for a year. This was effective, but it also was expensive. A company's management has to be fairly sure that there will be a significant payoff before investing that level of resources. Many companies, particularly those experimenting with underserved markets, will not be able to provide that level of resources.

What to Do in Underserved Markets

Partner with Organizations

Fortunately, many organizations are interested in spurring innovation in product and process development in underserved markets. A company can create a mutually beneficial partnership with one or more of these organizations to reduce the costs of gathering information, developing new products, and market-testing their attractiveness.

So, what kinds of organizations are these, why are they interested in spurring innovation, and what kinds of resources can they bring to a potential partnership? First, such organizations differ dramatically in type, but they share one common characteristic: they have the mission of improving services, jobs, and housing for underserved communities. In short, they "own the problem" of improving these communities. If you want to figure out which organization could be a potential partner for your company, just focus on the key challenges or issues that your products and services might address, and ask, "Who owns the problem? Which organization or agency has the mission of dealing with the challenge that my products and services can help address?" It could be a national nonprofit advocacy group, a local nonprofit service provider, an industry association, a municipal department, a federal agency, a research institution, a foundation, or even another firm serving the same market.

For example, the National Insurance Task Force described earlier in this chapter included many of these types of organizations in developing process innovations in the homeowner insurance market. At the national level, it included representatives from several insurance industry associations, a national nonprofit advocacy organization, insurance regulators, a university, a national foundation, and a number of corporations providing homeownership insurance. At the local level, the innovation was tested and refined through local partnerships including municipal departments, local nonprofit service providers, and local funders. While this arrangement is much more complex than most partnerships, it drives home an important point: there are many organizations that could potentially bring resources and information to your company as it seeks innovations in product and process for underserved markets.

Next, what kinds of resources can these potential partners bring to your company? Depending on the kind of organization, they can bring access to and information about underserved markets; they can bring funding, sometimes in cash but mostly in kind; they can identify test sites for product development and provide third-party evaluations of the innovations; and they can assist in the regulatory review and permitting process. Consider the following examples of how organizations brought each of these resources to their corporate partners:

Information and Access. Organizations that work extensively with underserved communities have often spent considerable time and effort gathering information on these markets that can be useful for product development. For example, in the Fannie Mae–Self-Help partnership described in Chapter 1, Self-Help had spent years studying the market for mortgages to low-income and low-wealth individuals. It had gathered a large dataset on the performances of these mortgages and had used its information to determine which particular product enhancements and service changes were required to profitably provide these mortgages. Such information was invaluable to Fannie Mae in determining how to develop a new program for purchasing mortgages for individuals in these populations.

TransFair USA brought a different kind of information to its partner, Green Mountain Coffee, described in Chapter 3. In this case, it had information on the consumers of coffee grown in underserved communities. Because it was working to expand demand among consumers for Fair Trade certified coffee, it also had a well-nuanced understanding of exactly which consumers were most interested in Fair Trade coffee, and most willing to pay a premium for the product. It was able to provide this information to Green Mountain Coffee, which helped it target the right customer segments for the launch of its line of Fair Trade certified coffees. This increased sales of Fair Trade coffee, thus helping TransFair further its mission.

Funding (Cash or In Kind). Nonprofit organizations, whether national or community-based, can serve as conduits through which funding to support research and development activities can flow. Funding from the Ford Foundation helped to strengthen Self-Help's balance sheet. This let it take on a portion of Fannie Mae's financial risk in testing out the new product. Similarly, funding provided to microfinance institutions in India is enabling them to take on a portion of ICICI Bank's financial risk (see Chapter 3). In both cases, the funding makes it possible to test the new product and determine the true level of financial risk involved. Also in both cases, it would have been very difficult for the foundations and government agencies involved to provide funding directly to the corporation. Having the nonprofit involved makes it easier for a foundation or government agency to provide the funding, because it helps ensure that the money will be used in ways that benefit the residents of underserved communities.

Nonprofits can also provide valuable services in kind. For example, in the partnership between Manpower and its nonprofit partners, (see Introduction and Chapter 2), there is no financial guarantee or funding. Rather, the nonprofits provide training services to individuals that Manpower is going to place into jobs. These are provided entirely in kind. In fact, these are services that the nonprofits already provide to individuals in the underserved communities. The only difference is that the individuals are chosen according to criteria jointly developed by Manpower and the nonprofit to ensure that they can be placed by Manpower at the end of the training period.

Product Testing. Organizations that provide services and organize networks in underserved communities often have extensive contacts with members of those communities and can easily find opportunities to test products and services under development. This access can speed the process and lower the costs of the development of the products and services. In the IBM example noted earlier in this chapter, IBM chose to work with SeniorNet because it had a network of 240 learning centers across the United States. These were ideal locations for IBM to test its Web-accessibility product. SeniorNet also provided staffing for the testing process, further lowering IBM's product development costs. SeniorNet did this because the product would create significant benefits for its constituents. It was able to engage its constituents in the product testing process precisely because they saw that the product would be useful to them and to their peers. There are many examples of other companies where nonprofit organizations and their constituents have served essentially as continuous focus groups, providing steady feedback to their partners as the products and services were developed over time.

Regulatory Review and Permitting. Businesses can work with partners to speed the process of regulatory review and permitting for product development. This is particularly true for partners drawn from regulatory agencies or standard-setting organizations. When these organizations partner with businesses, they can provide invaluable guidance on what kinds of product and service features will likely meet quick regulatory approval, and what kinds will drag on forever. They also can carry the message to their peers that the product development is intended to be a win-win for both communities and business. Hearing support for a new product or service approach from their peers sometimes reduces the skepticism or caution that might otherwise be evoked from regulators.

The National Insurance Task Force provides a good example of this. In the United States, homeownership insurance is regulated on a state-by-state basis. The National Insurance Task Force partnered with the Departments of Insurance from a number of states. These regulators were able to help the National Insurance Task Force companies understand in considerable detail the kinds of product and process developments that would likely trouble regulators, as well as the ones that regulators would regard with greater favor. They also helped spread information to their peers about the approaches that were being tried, and they brought back information about regulatory reactions to the working groups. This feedback guided the development of the product and process improvements and helped to avoid wasting time pursuing avenues that were unlikely to meet with regulatory approval.

It's equally important to understand what the potential partners need from the business for the partnership to be a success for them. Sometimes the answer is obvious: funding. But often there are other nonfinancial factors that are equally important: for example, public visibility, political alliances, intellectual property, and increased hiring or purchasing from local communities. For partners from the academic world, access to information, as well as the right to use it in research, may be the most important resource that the partnership can provide. For example, one partnership was seeking a third-party evaluator to track and analyze the results of the partnership activities. A regional university was so interested in being able to conduct research on the project that it was willing to raise most of the funds itself needed for the evaluation—provided that the partners would allow it to use the information as the basis of a research paper.

Partnerships between corporations and organizations that are trying to develop new products and services for underserved markets do have some predictable tensions. A typical one is the tension between the desire of the corporation to keep a good market to itself, and the desire of its partnering organization to spread the new product or process as far and wide as possible. This tension can manifest itself in a number of ways. The first involves confidentiality and trade secrets. Generally, the corporate partner will want to keep the details of the product and process improvements confidential. The corporation has invested time and money to create an improvement that has given it a competitive edge over other participants in the market. Why would it turn around and give away information about that improvement for free? On the other hand, the nonprofit or governmental partner is investing in the product development because it wants to generate benefits for the community. It would like to post all the details on the Internet and feature them at trade shows. The more corporations that provide the improved product or service, the better.

This tension, and others like it, must be recognized and managed. Different partnerships often arrive at different solutions. One typical solution is to agree that the details will be confidential for a fixed period—say, one or two years. After that time, the details will be released. Another solution is to agree to an evaluation that provides an in-depth analysis of the innovation and its result after a fixed period. A third approach is to agree to make some information and the results available to be shared widely, and to keep another portion of the information confidential.

■ 5. IMPROVE THE ENABLING ENVIRONMENT

What's Different about Underserved Markets

The enabling environment can stifle innovation. To function well, the innovation process must be free to follow interesting ideas and exciting market opportunities. It must be able to test out new approaches and abandon or shift them quickly if they are not working well. It must be nimble and responsive to the changes in the marketplace.

Certain aspects of the enabling environment can make all of that difficult. Laws and regulations can (1) require that businesses engage with certain communities, and (2) prescribe the form of the engagement. This can dampen the enthusiasm for innovation. In many companies, the compliance unit takes over the mandatory engagement, making sure that the company is following the letter of the law. But this rarely leads to any type of productive innovation. Mandated engagement becomes an isolated unit—it's a requirement, not an opportunity.

Well-intentioned laws and regulations can also have unintended consequences. For example, the company may be forbidden by regulation from gathering data on the gender or race of the individuals to whom it provides products and services. This type of regulation is often enacted to ensure that products and services are provided without regard to race or gen-

---

What's different?

- Company may view engagement with underserved community just as a matter of compliance.

What to do about it.

- Turn mandated community engagement into low-cost information-gathering opportunity.
- Seek external support to share cost of innovation and experimentation.

der. But it may also have the unintended side effect of making it impossible for the company to track how well it is doing in reaching particular underserved market segments. Because the company can't track the characteristics of the people buying the product, it can't know whether or not product innovations are doing a better (or worse) job of reaching particular underserved markets.

Similarly, regulations exerting control over pricing may have been enacted with the laudable intent of ensuring that everyone pays the same price and no one pays an exorbitant price. This is the case for regulations for financial services and insurance. But it also can have unintended consequences. It can mean that a company has little incentive to innovate for some parts of the underserved market, which are higher cost than others, because it can't raise prices to address the costs of these market segments or to recover the cost of innovation. These market segments may then end up being filled by "fringe institutions"—institutions that offer narrowly focused products and services that meet the customers' needs, but at a much higher price or lower quality.

What to Do in Underserved Markets

Managers who are responsible for the innovation process can dramatically shift the relationship with the enabling environment, turning it from a liability into an asset. Indeed, the enabling environment can become a force that helps propel the development of innovations rather than dampening them. There are two key strategies for achieving this result: (1) turn mandated engagement with underserved communities into low-cost information-gathering opportunities, and (2) engage the enabling environment to provide funding to support innovation.

Turn Mandated Engagement into Low-cost Information-gathering Opportunities

There are many industries in which regulations mandate engagement with specific underserved communities. This is particularly true for industries such as healthcare, utilities, finance, and insurance. Regulations might mandate that a particular level of service be provided to customers in certain underserved markets. Regulations also might require that companies provide regular forums for the airing of issues and concerns regarding products and services supplied to particular customer segments.

Often, companies facing such requirements respond by developing special units to address the needs and interests of these communities. These are not considered part of the "mainstream" business by the company. Meeting the standards for compliance by engaging with these communities is seen as part of the cost of doing business. What management looks for from these units is the assurance that the company is in compliance. The goal is to achieve superior compliance with minimal cost. These units are not expected to generate innovations, and it's not clear that their innovations would be taken terribly seriously if they did.

However, it is possible to turn this perspective on its head by framing the mandated engagement as a low-cost opportunity to gather information that is useful for innovation. The company has to engage with these communities to meet its regulatory requirements. Engaging with the communities will generate information about their needs and interests. The question becomes, then, how to capture the information in a way that is useful for innovation and gets it to the right spots within the company.

Verizon's Community Affairs Team. Verizon's work with its Community Affairs Team provides a good example. It has positioned its Community Affairs Team as a crucial point of contact for communicating between specific consumer segments and relevant business units, establishing a mechanism for driving changes to enhance new products and services for these consumer segments, including elderly, non-English-speaking, low-income, and disabled customers.

The Community Affairs Team works through Verizon's Consumer Advisory Panels (CAPs), which are mandated mechanisms for engaging with underserved communities that are required by regulation. The CAPs were created by Verizon (then NYNEX) in the early 1990s in response to regulatory requirements. The purpose of the CAPs is to provide a discussion forum on issues of mutual concern to the company and stakeholder groups. Each CAP comprises local community representatives from the nonprofit, private, and public sectors. Members advocate on behalf of their "special needs" constituency groups: the elderly, disabled individuals, low-income, and non-English-speaking customers.

Many regulated companies have groups that are equivalent to Verizon's CAPs, and most of them do not link their groups into the product and process innovation cycle. Verizon approached the relationship with its CAPs in a different way. It saw that they could provide useful information on the needs and interests of a range of market niches. The Community Affairs Team was tasked with gathering information about how well (or poorly) particular products and services are working in these market niches, and about innovations that could improve the product or service. This information was then channeled to the appropriate business units for improving the product and services. As a result, Verizon's business units have been able to draw on the CAP information to drive quality and timeliness, as well as to increase the utility of new products and services for specific market niches in underserved communities. These efforts have led to improvements in products such as directory services, voice dialing, white pages, and automated operator services (Sabapathy et al., 2003).

Vodacom Community Service Program. Vodacom, the largest provider of telephone service in South Africa, provides another example of how a company can turn mandated engagement with underserved communities into an opportunity for innovation. Like many telephone companies, Vodacom is required to provide basic phone services to underserved communities. In addition, the price for these services, which is mandated by law, is well below commercial rates. Most telephone companies accept the "fact" that mandated coverage at minimum prices to underserved communities will not be profitable, so they offer a stripped-down version of their standard service and cross-subsidize the costs with profits from other customers. Unlike these companies, Vodacom was able to connect mandated engagement to its innovation process and develop a profitable approach to providing these services.

Vodacom decided to build on the fact that its cellular infrastructure provided coverage for 93 percent of South Africa's population.

Through its engagement with underserved communities, it also was aware both of the pressing need to generate jobs in these communities, and of the entrepreneurial nature of many of the residents. Building on these insights, it developed a Community Services program to provide cellular telephone service to disadvantaged and underserved South African communities while creating opportunities for entrepreneurs. Under this program, the company establishes entrepreneur-owned "phone shops" in townships and other disadvantaged communities by offering prospective business owners five cellular lines at a cost of about U.S. $4,000 per franchise. The company also provides converted shipping containers to house the businesses. These containers, emblazoned with the corporate logo, promote brand recognition as well as a lost-cost site option. Community members can use the cellular phones for U.S. $0.11, a cost much lower than prepaid phone alternatives. Shop owners retain one third of the revenue; at most shops, entrepreneurs can cover their costs and make a profit from this rate.

The program has generated a profitable business for Vodacom and better services for these underserved communities. When it was started in 1994, the Community Services program was subsidized by the company, but it now generates enough revenue to cover its costs from sales. As of 2003, the program provided over 23,000 cellular lines in 4,400 locations. It offers a vital, but once unavailable, service to a new market of disadvantaged customers while generating revenue for the company. The program also creates thousands of job opportunities for entrepreneurs (Reck and Wood, 2003).

Engage Enabling Environment to Provide Funding to Support Innovation

Laws, regulations, and government agencies—all part of the enabling environment—may be seen by managers responsible for product development as a source of delay and "red tape." Managers may complain about bureaucratic meddling and the complexity of the regulatory and permitting process. But the enabling environment can also be a source of support and resources for business innovation. In the United States, there has been a long history of public policy that has helped businesses build products and services for the middle-income market. When business goals align with the goals of regulators and lawmakers, the possibility of dramatic business innovation supported by policy and government assistance is opened up.

The market for housing production and home mortgages provides many examples of this. Federal policy has long promoted homeownership as an important goal. Policies such as home mortgage deductibility and the creation of Fannie Mae helped build and widen the market for homeownership among the middle class. Similarly, regulations enabling the securitization of home mortgages set the stage for an explosion of innovation in home mortgage products and also for the development of a wealth of attractive investment products based on home mortgages.

Federal laws and policies have also created the incentives for business to develop products and services for underserved markets. In the affordable housing industry, one of the most important federal laws has been the Low Income Housing Tax Credit (LIHTC). Created by the Tax Reform Act of 1986, the LIHTC program gives states the equivalent of nearly $5 billion in annual budget authority to issue tax credits for the acquisition, rehabilitation, or new construction of rental housing targeted to lower-income households. Since its inception, the LIHTC has enabled business to provide financing for nearly 22,000 projects and more than 1,141,000 housing units. The LIHTC has facilitated business innovation in many aspects of the process, including financing, acquisition, construction, and management (U.S. Department of Housing and Urban Development, 2005).

Innovation in affordable housing is not limited to financing for construction. For-profit owners and managers of affordable housing have been working with nonprofit organizations to develop resources and regulations that would permit them to wire up their units for high-speed Internet access. The nonprofits have been successful in persuading regulators of affordable housing in several states to provide greater incentive for the owners and operators of the housing to wire up existing units. More important, they also have been successful in developing government resources to support increased access to the Internet in these units. With government assistance, nonprofits and businesses together launched "access@home" in 2005, a $1 billion initiative that is in the process of building more than 15,000 affordable homes with high-speed digital Internet connectivity and provide low-income families personal access to computers and technology services. Residents in each of these properties have high-speed digital access and a package of Internet-related services, including computer purchase vouchers, computer training for residents, and a community-specific Web site that provides information about personal finance, health, schools, jobs, childcare, and other services. This initiative is a good example of how the enabling environment can be tapped for resources that provide the support needed for business innovation in creating and delivering products and services to an underserved market (One Economy, 2005).

These examples show that it is possible for federal policies, regulations, and funding to be developed in ways that help businesses innovate to better serve underserved communities. But how can *your business* determine whether there are potential ways to work with government to shape policy, regulation, and funding to enable you to better serve these markets?

The answer to this question returns to the core message of the book: if you can create a *win-win relationship* between your government and the appropriate government agency or legislative committee, there is an opportunity to shape policy, regulation, and funding. To determine whether this is possible, ask yourself the following questions: "If my business could innovate to better serve underserved markets, would I be making voters significantly better off? How?" If the answer is "Yes, because they would have more income and assets," there is a significant opportunity to create a win-win relationship with government. If the answer is "Yes, because they would have more fashionable clothes and better consumer goods," the task of creating a win-win relationship will be harder.

Once you have determined whether there is the potential of a win-win relationship, you will need to find out which government agencies and legislative committees are the right partners. In general, these will be bodies that are trying to create similar benefits to the ones that your company can deliver to these markets. In the example above, the owners and managers of affordable housing identified that the regulators were interested in the same benefit—

Internet access—that they wanted to provide. This was the basis for crafting a win-win relationship.

MEASURING PROGRESS

What measures can help you track and manage innovation in process and product that is accelerated through engagement with underserved markets? This can be a complex question, as responsibility for innovating in product and process is often located in different functional areas in different companies. Some companies, such as Hewlett-Packard and IBM, have specific units charged with developing new products and services. Other companies locate the responsibility for innovation in their marketing units. Still others locate it in the brand management and product management areas.

As a result of this diversity of location, there are a wide variety of measures that companies use to evaluate their progress and success in developing innovative products and processes. However, some are quite commonly used. A number of these indicators are quantitative, such as:

- percentage of sales coming from new products and services
- percentage of profits coming from new products and services
- time to market
- number of patents

Some indicators, however, are qualitative:

- Did the company identify market opportunities, accurately assess whether they were potentially lucrative, and develop ways of commercializing them faster than its competitors?
- Did the company correctly assess which market opportunities were *not* lucrative and, accordingly, not waste time and money dealing with them?

In addition to these measures for all markets, some measures are unique to innovation and product development for underserved markets. Executives responsible for this activity need to measure and manage how information from, and interaction with, underserved markets helps increase innovation in product and process. The indicators that they track typically include both quantitative and qualitative measures.

They track output from innovation teams that interact with underserved communities or include community representation in the innovation process. How many and what kinds of innovations are being created? How well have these innovations been accepted in the marketplace? What impact have these innovations had on costs or revenues? Managers also need to capture and promote stories showing best practices, to help these migrate throughout the company.

Managers need to be aware of, and promote, the ways in which interacting with underserved communities can foster creativity and innovation across all the company's business lines. This information will likely be in anecdotal form—stories about how insights from underserved communities were transferred to other parts of the company to spark innovations in process or product. The examples mentioned above on how Hewlett-Packard's work in Kuppam helped spur innovation in the way that digital photography is marketed to the middle-income consumer in India (see Chapter 1) and how IBM's work with SeniorNet helped it develop Web-accessibility products for all customers (earlier in this chapter), highlight the importance of anecdotal information. Although the impact is not easily quantifiable, the anecdotes help managers to understand where the impact is occurring and how to support and enhance it over time.

PUTTING IT ALL TOGETHER: CASE STUDY

Four of the five success strategies described in this chapter can be found in this case study of Russell Simmons, the hip-hop entrepreneur who founded Def Jam Records and Phat Fashions, and his company's experience in launching the RushCard, a prepaid debit card aimed at the 48 million "unbanked" Americans.

■ 1. MINE AND TRANSLATE LOCAL INFORMATION

Russell Simmons and his colleagues at Rush Communications, his media holding company, had an intimate knowledge of consumers in underserved markets. Simmons himself and many of his managers came from underserved communities. In addition, many customers for Def Jam Records and Phat Fashions are from these communities.

The need for a better payment mechanism for underserved communities came into clear view for Simmons and his colleagues when their customers identified the need for a mechanism to enable them to buy Phat Fashion products online. Many customers didn't have or weren't able to get credit cards, which made it difficult to make purchases online. Simmons recognized that by enabling customers to make these purchases without resorting to expensive C.O.D. or money order options, Phat Fashions could develop a wider audience and capture more direct sales.

Rush Communications began its quest to develop a better financial product for its "unbanked" customers because it wanted to solve an internal payment issue for existing lines of business. It also had access to information about its unbanked customers—"local market information." The company compiled all the requests and features its target customers were looking for and set out to develop the RushCard program. Only later, as the company explored further needs of the market, did it see the opportunity to build an additional profit-making business by expanding the company's focus to the needs of consumers beyond its own current and future customers.

In addition to information about its own unbanked customers, Rush had experience selling a product similar to the stored value card it was proposing. Rush Communications and Russell Simmons had been approached numerous times by telephone service providers who wanted access to a unique, targeted group of consumers that relied on phone cards. Rush wanted to know why consumers would pay significantly higher rates to use a phone card to make local telephone calls rather than use their own phones. The company found that some consumers used the cards mainly to obtain lower rates for international calls. Many others, however, lacking credit cards, bank accounts, or credit records, could not gain access to home or mobile telephone service and were relying on pay phones for daily telecommunications needs. In order to launch its own prepaid mobile telecommunications services, Rush had to contend with the same lack of credit records and banking relationships of these consumers. Rush developed Rush Mobile, a phone card aimed at this market, and had good experience in selling the card profitably.

■ 2. ADAPT BUSINESS MODEL TO COMMUNITY REALITIES

Before starting to develop the RushCard program, Simmons approached major banks to attempt to convince them to develop products to help consumers without access to traditional banking services, but he found little interest. Many mainstream financial institutions had tried and failed to provide services to the unbanked. The companies either could not develop products that adequately met consumer needs or were unable to achieve the margins of their more conventional businesses.

Traditional banks also faced technological hurdles to developing a prepaid value card. These financial institutions relied on legacy systems that were built for checking and credit card processing. They had increasingly outsourced their processing to third parties that could not accommodate the requirements for implementing prepaid card programs. Simmons realized that he would need to develop an entirely new processing platform focused solely on prepaid cards if he was to succeed in developing a profitable product.

■ 3. CHANGE INTERNAL INCENTIVES AND CHALLENGE CULTURAL ASSUMPTIONS

In this case, there was not a need to change internal incentives or challenge cultural assumptions. The company's internal incentives already provided support for engaging with these markets, and the managers were quite familiar with the markets.

■ 4. CREATE PARTNERSHIPS AND STRATEGIC ALLIANCES

Rush Communications teamed up with Unifund, an institutional debt collection company, to form UniRush Financial Services. UniRush launched the Rush Prepaid Visa Card in March 2003 (the "Rush-Card"). The card, issued by the Manufacturers and Traders Trust Company (M&T Bank), can be funded by direct deposit of customers' payroll or government benefits or through three other methods of funds transfer. Customers pay a one-time enrollment fee and a per transaction fee with a monthly cap. The RushCard can be used like a debit card for purchases, to obtain cash at ATMs, or for bill payment.

By the end of 2005, more than 500,000 individuals had signed up for the RushCard. The average income of a RushCard holder is around $26,000 per year, and the average age is 24. UniRush has found that many of its customers use the RushCard during transitional periods in their lives.

The company has faced criticism from consumer groups and others who compare its charges unfavorably to those for basic checking accounts that banks are required to offer by statute. UniRush maintains that the more appropriate comparison, under which it performs favorably, is with check-cashing services that can average almost twice the RushCard's average annual fees of $180 per year. The Center for Financial Services Innovation, an initiative of ShoreBank Advisory Services, with support from the Ford Foundation, recently published a white paper, "Stored Value Cards: A Scan of Current Trends and Future Opportunities" (Jacobs, 2004). The report notes the difficulty of making comparisons of the costs of stored value cards, basic checking-account, and check-cashing services depending on the pricing structure of the stored value card in question, the types and frequency of transactions, and charges for overdrafts and bounced checks associated with checking accounts.

UniRush is continually monitoring the needs of its customers to develop additional services. The company believes that by providing information and educating its cardholders, it can build an even more profitable business. For example, UniRush began to educate its cardholders about the fact that while many of them were eligible for earned income tax credits (EITC), over $2 billion was left unclaimed each year because of failure to file tax returns. In 2005, the company teamed up with Intuit, the providers of TurboTax, to offer Rush-Card customers the ability to file their taxes online and have refunds or EITC credited directly to their RushCard. Now, UniRush is working with the large credit bureaus to explore how an alternative scoring system could be developed to take account of customers' experience with prepaid cards.

■ 5. IMPROVE THE ENABLING ENVIRONMENT

In a reverse of the usual process by which companies address social problems, Russell Simmons is building on his commercial experience with the unbanked to use philanthropy to improve financial literacy in the inner cities. The Hip Hop Summit Action Network, founded by Simmons and others in the hip hop industry to register and educate voters, launched a series of high-profile summit meetings in 2005 for young people on financial literacy and empowerment. Sponsored by Chrysler Financial and Anheuser-Busch, the summits feature financial experts and celebrities from the sporting, television, and music industries engaging with youth on topics covering financial literacy, basic banking, repairing and understanding credit scores, asset and wealth management, auto loans, homeownership, and entrepreneurship. Simmons, as chairman of the Hip Hop Summit Action Network, played a critical role in developing the new focus of the organization for the years between presidential elections (when voter registration is a less compelling issue). Improving the financial literacy of this audience will both improve their lives and also make them savvier consumers for Rush's financial products (Marshall, 2005).

■ CONCLUSION ■

Companies can accelerate strategic innovations in process and product by changing the way their innovation teams engage with underserved communities. This process can create new market opportunities in both undeserved communities and mainstream markets.

Creating strategic innovations that open up new markets typically requires deep engagement with those markets. It requires managers to put together process and product in entirely new ways, see new patterns, or engage in "out of the box" thinking. Managers must sift through potential new ideas for these markets rapidly to find the ones that are worth developing and testing.

However, many innovation teams in large companies have little or no engagement with underserved communities. The managers that work with these communities are often isolated within HR, government affairs, or community relations. As such, they are rarely connected to teams charged with innovation. This isolation significantly increases the difficulty of creating strategic innovations because the innovation teams don't have access to a deep understanding of these markets.

Companies address this challenge by pursuing a variety of strategies to connect managers responsible for innovation with information about underserved markets. They make sure that individuals with deep experience in these markets are included on innovation teams. They create opportunities for managers from these teams to immerse themselves in underserved markets. They create internal incentives for partnerships between innovation teams and departments who interact with those markets. Finally, they create partnerships with, or purchase, companies that are innovating successfully in these markets. All of these approaches make the company better able to develop strategic innovations for underserved markets.

By engaging innovation teams with underserved markets successfully, your company can create new products and services that have significant markets and limited competition. Underserved communities benefit as well because they get products and services that both better meet their needs and are more affordable.

For additional case studies and further details, see the following websites:

Base of the Pyramid Protocol: www.bus.umich.edu/BOP-Protocol/project overview.htm
Center for Corporate Citizenship at Boston College: www.bcccc.net
Next Billion: www.nextbillion.net
Win-Win Partners: www.winwinpartner.com

5

BUILDING PARTNERSHIPS
THAT WORK

In this chapter, we describe when a partnership can be helpful as well as the do's and don'ts of getting started and managing a partnership. We provide specific advice on (1) how to structure a partnership so that it is truly a win-win relationship for both sides; (2) the critical issues that must be addressed at start-up for a partnership to succeed; and (3) strategies for managing a partnership—including deciding when and how to end one.

This chapter is structured differently from the previous four. Those were organized around the five success factors, and "creating alliances and partnerships" was one of the factors. This chapter is organized around how to create and maintain a partnership that works well. Accordingly, it focuses first on why creating and maintaining mutually beneficial partnerships deserves management attention. It then focuses on the characteristics of successful partnerships, how to start them, and how to maintain them over time.

CREATING AND MAINTAINING PARTNERSHIPS DESERVE MANAGEMENT ATTENTION

Why give special attention to partnerships? There are three important reasons. First, win-win partnerships are the core of many successful strategies for working in underserved markets. In fact, although "creating alliances and partnerships" is one of the five success factors, it can actually help you to achieve each of the other four success factors as well. Second, partnerships are increasingly becoming part of "business as usual." Third, partnering is challenging! It takes special attention, talent, and effort to make partnerships work. Each reason is addressed in turn in this section.

Partnerships Are Essential to Implementing Strategies in Underserved Markets

At the outset of this book, we emphasized that *a win-win relationship is everything*. To succeed in creating long-term business value, companies must also create long-term community value. Partnerships are an important tool for helping to create long-term community value.

Partnerships can help you implement each of the other four success factors explored throughout this book. The right partner can expeditiously *mine and translate local market information*. For example, managers at Green Mountain Coffee Roasters expressed skepticism at the potential demand for fair-trade coffee. TransFair provided data and information that showed how concerned students across the United States were championing fair-trade coffee and launching campaigns to influence the policies of university purchasing departments. This helped Green Mountain's managers to see how the demand for fair-trade coffee was beginning to emerge (Center for Corporate Citizenship, 2004a).

A partner can provide unique guidance that helps a company *adapt its business model to community realities*. This is how Operation Hope has helped Union Bank of California. Investing in a check-cashing operation is extremely controversial. Many critics accuse these businesses of gouging low-wage workers by charging excessive fees. Operation Hope performed a critical role to help Union Bank build a business model that enabled its low-wage consumers to become better managers of their finances and helped these individuals "convert" into viable customers for traditional banking services (Center for Corporate Citizenship, 2004a).

In the United States, nonprofits increasingly serve as the engine of innovative thinking and programs related to education, health, and community and economic development. In many instances, the innovative talent of nonprofits can translate into exciting win-win opportunities. For example, Self-Help has helped Fannie Mae to develop new products that serve the lower-income market and provide greater access to housing. Working Today has created a model to provide health insurance to temporary workers (Ford Foundation, 2005).

A partner can inspire a company to *change internal incentives and challenge cultural assumptions.* For example, Manpower's nonprofit partners helped its staff to change their understanding of the job-readiness of candidates from underserved markets, and to see new opportunities to provide services both to its current clients and to new markets as well.

And partners can help to *improve the enabling environment.* In Chapter 2, we shared the experience of Metropolis 2020. This Chicago-land partnership of business, nonprofits, and government agencies had the combined credibility and authority to influence the creation of a state affordable-housing tax credit that matches an employer's contributions to affordable housing dollar for dollar. Working alone, it would have been difficult for any single business or nonprofit to influence this policy (Ford Foundation, 2005).

The lesson is clear. You need a partner to do well. And you need a partner to do good. Win-win partnerships help both your company and its important communities to focus on creating strategies that generate long-term value for both the business and the individuals that reside in underserved markets. In short, partners keep your business focused on delivering both sides of a win-win proposition.

Partnerships Are Increasingly Becoming Part of "Business as Usual"

Partnership has become an increasing part of core business operations. Competitors form collaborative joint ventures. Businesses from entirely different industries find innovative opportunity by working on projects together. By extension, leading thinkers in business see great opportunities in partnering with nonprofits and government. Many believe that partnerships among business, nonprofits, and government agencies (often called "cross-sector partnerships") will become more common.

In fact, 38 percent of a sample of executives from 515 small, medium, and large U.S. businesses say they have formed partnerships with local nonprofit organizations; 22 percent have formed partnerships with national nonprofits; 20 percent have formed partnerships with state and government agencies. And 11 percent have formed partnerships with federal agencies (Center for Corporate Citizenship, 2004b). While it is unlikely that all of these fit the criteria of win-win partnerships, the numbers do indicate that collaborative relationships among companies, nonprofits, and government agencies are indeed becoming a part of the landscape.

More and more of these partnerships are forming to address important and complicated problems that are too challenging for any one institution to solve by itself. Companies, nonprofits, and governments have formed partnerships on a wide range of global issues from HIV-AIDS (the Global Business Coalition on HIV-AIDS), to preserving fish stocks (the Marine Stewardship Council), to increasing road safety (the Global Road Safety Partnership). Respected global institutions like the World Bank have invested extensive resources to develop and promote partnerships that engage business in supporting community and economic development through its Business Partners for Development program. In the United States, Canada, and Europe, numerous partnerships tackle issues such as education, crime, affordable housing, and at-risk youth. Regions such as Cleveland, Ohio; Newark, New Jersey; Benton Harbor, Michigan; and Racine, Wisconsin have all formed regional partnerships including business, government, and non-profit members to support sustainable and inclusive community development.

Partnering Is Challenging

In most instances, managing a successful partnership to implement an underserved markets strategy requires special skills, competencies, and relationships. More often than not, the partnerships that make underserved markets strategies work are not run-of-the-mill joint ventures with other companies. Instead, such partnerships typically involve teaming up with strange bedfellows—nonprofit organizations. This approach succeeds for companies as diverse as retailers, heavy manufacturers, financial institutions, and high-tech information communication technology companies.

Forming partnerships with nonprofit organizations that specialize in the issue of community and economic development makes sense for numerous reasons. These organizations possess knowledge of underserved markets. They have experience working in these markets. They possess networks that connect to a wide range of influential individuals living in underserved communities. They have earned the trust of these individuals. They possess their own "brand reputation" among the constituents that benefit from their services. And they often offer extraordinary technical expertise on topics— for example, how to train and prepare a qualified workforce—that can create value for business and society alike.

But partnerships are not easy. Companies and nonprofit partners can both literally and figuratively speak different languages. Whereas your company is highly focused on the goals of generating revenue, controlling costs, and building market share, a nonprofit partner is equally focused on different goals, like building the skills of individuals who lack a high school diploma, improving health for recent immigrants, providing shelter for the homeless, and influencing public policy to support community development. Whereas large companies have state-of-the-art information and communications systems, rigorous performance management processes, a sizeable and talented staff, and capital to invest, many nonprofits possess a lean staff and limited budget. It's not uncommon for a nonprofit to work hand-to-mouth.

What's more, nonprofit organizations and typical for-profit companies often maintain very strong stereotypes about one another. Research shows that nonprofit executives are quite suspicious of their counterparts in companies. They believe corporate executives do not value their work. Some believe that corporate executives may even oppose the work and mission of most community and economic development nonprofits. In contrast, corporate executives often feel frustrated by their nonprofit colleagues. They worry that nonprofits are only interested in gaining access to the company's money. Some believe that most nonprofits would prefer to see the company go out of business (Laufer, Green, Isaac, 2004).

Building successful partnerships takes work, but the effort pays off. Win-win partnerships are a critical success factor to finding untapped assets in underserved markets. See the box on page 181 for a wide range of examples of organizations that have successfully partnered with business.

CHARACTERISTICS OF SUCCESSFUL PARTNERSHIPS

What constitutes a true win-win partnership? First, let's consider what win-win partnerships are *not*. They are not transactional. A relationship in which a company makes a grant to a nonprofit is not a win-win partnership. A relationship in which one partner provides a proprietary service to the other for a fee is not a win-win partnership.

Successful partnerships share certain features: shared goals and objectives, mutual expectations to produce specific products and services for all partners, division of labor and resources, explicit agreements (either formal or informal), and commitment to a long-term relationship.

Shared Goals and Objectives

Win-win partnerships establish common goals and objectives. Operation Hope and Union Bank share the goal to get more people "banked." These goals are perfectly aligned. However, some partners may share goals that, while not perfectly aligned, are highly complementary. For example, Hindustan Lever's goals are to get more personal hygiene product distributed in underserved markets. To do so, it has established relationships with grassroots partners that have the goal of providing sustainable, income-generating opportunities for women. Building from these goals, the partners have formed strategies to create opportunities for women to serve as the sales and distribution force for Lever's products.

Mutual Expectations to Produce Deliverables for All Partners

Each member of a win-win partnership takes on the responsibility to help the other achieve the critical results it is aiming for. For example, Green Mountain Coffee Roasters has become a champion of the fair-trade coffee movement. At the same time, its partner, TransFair, helps Green Mountain to sell its Fair Trade certified coffee profitably.

Management Tips: Potential Partners

Nonprofits

1. Local
   - local community development groups
   - churches and religious organizations
   - unions
   - membership organizations (e.g., Kiwanis, Rotary)
   - community colleges and universities
2. National and International
   - national interest-based groups (e.g., National Urban League, National Council of La Raza)
   - consumer organizations (e.g., Fair Trade, Co-op America)
   - national economic development organizations (e.g., Jobs for the Future)
   - social and environmental organizations (e.g., Oxfam, Conservation International)
   - international private voluntary organizations (e.g., CARE)
   - foundations
   - policy institutes (e.g., Brookings)
   - global multi-stakeholder initiatives (e.g., Ethical Trading Initiative)

Government

1. Local
   - city agencies, including schools, police, and firefighters
   - high schools and community colleges
   - traditional leaders (e.g., tribal chiefs)
   - workforce development boards
2. National or International
   - state and national agencies (e.g., U.S. Department of Labor)
   - embassies
   - United Nations (UNIDO, UNDP, International Labor Organization)
   - bilateral and multilateral donors

Business

   - peer companies
   - financial institutions
   - local, national, and international business associations (e.g., chambers)
   - global business initiatives (e.g., Global Compact)

Source: Simanis et al., 2005.

The partners in Metropolis 2020 are dedicated to building a stronger metro Chicago in ways that can benefit each of the partners.

Division of Labor and Resources

It's important for each partner to make a commitment of money, resources, or time. While supporting a partnership's budget requirement is important, it is often more valuable for partners to provide talented staff, skills, and competencies. For example, Manpower's distinctive TechReach partnership model brings an established team of service providers—from the company, local community-based organizations, community colleges, city agencies, and local employers—to collectively own a project. Community organizations contribute their knowledge of, and access to, local community labor pools, experience in providing social services, and relationships with local government and civil sector funding agencies. Community colleges have experience with technical curriculum design and delivery to local populations. Local employers offer guidance on specific positions they are trying to fill, providing the promise of actual employment to program graduates. Without partners, Manpower would be forced to confront a steep learning curve in replicating this knowledge and experience internally (Center for Corporate Citizenship, 2003).

Explicit Agreements (Formal or Informal)

Win-win partnerships are formalized through clear agreements. Often, partners develop formal memoranda of understanding or other forms of agreement. However, it's not always necessary to get it in writing. Marriott's partnership with the Kauai Food Bank proceeded according to the norms of Hawaiian Island culture—through discussion that reaches consensus, but not written agreement or formal contract; nevertheless, expectations, deliverables, and roles for each partner are well defined through the discussion process (Center for Corporate Citizenship, 2002).

Commitment to a Long-Term Relationship

Organizations that build successful partnerships set an objective to work together over the long term. Of course, this doesn't mean sticking with a partnership that isn't working. Nor does it mean that an organization should walk away at the first setback or after the first success. In their respective partnerships with Capital Area Training Foundation and Goodwill, both AMD and TJX experienced similar challenges when the economic downturn in 2001 caused falling revenues and increasing pressure to reduce headcount. Suddenly, the immediate goal to hire individuals from underserved communities came under threat. However, rather than end the partnership, each entity worked with its partner to modify goals and objectives to weather the storm and continue to support training and development.

Together, these key attributes define a win-win partnership. The next section provides guidance on how to make such partnerships work.

■ STARTING UP A WIN-WIN PARTNERSHIP

There are five steps that your company should follow from the outset to build a successful partnership:

1. Know yourself—motives matter.
2. The vision thing.
3. Do the due diligence.
4. Build the relationship.
5. Build organizational capacity.

1. Know Yourself—Motives Matter

In our research, we heard a story about a funeral home in a major city on the West Coast. The funeral home offered to partner with a local elementary school to build a computer learning center. And in return, the funeral home asked that the school help sell the services of the funeral home to the grandparents of every student!

Clearly, this is not the kind of partnership anyone would want to promote. Such a relationship is at best transactional—you scratch my back and I'll scratch yours. At worst, it manipulates the pressing needs of children and community to deliver profitable gain.

Motives matter in forming partnerships. Being clear with yourself and with your partner is essential. There is another story about a large insurance company that approached an inner-city nonprofit community development corporation to build a partnership. When asked what they wanted from the partnership, the team of managers from the insurance company made a long and impassioned speech about serving communities in need, giving back, and helping inner cities to thrive. The nonprofit didn't buy a word of it. The company had traditionally resisted every entreaty to help these communities. Why was it so interested now? Why the change of heart? The nonprofit said thanks but no thanks.

In truth, the company was coming under extraordinary pressure from activists because of its practices that appeared to discriminate by race and ethnicity. What it really wanted from a partnership was not a way to give back; rather, it wanted a way to address critics, improve its own performance, and generate good PR. Hat in hand, the managers returned and told the nonprofit what was really motivating their interest in the partnership. The nonprofit's reaction: thanks for letting us know, and let's get to work!

If partners aren't clear about their motives, at best they will start off on the wrong foot and compromise the ability of the partnership to succeed. At worst they may pursue work that generates a "lose-lose" outcome for the business and the community.

Motives don't necessarily need to start out as purely altruistic. Hindustan Lever and CEMEX clearly pursue their partnerships with the intent of generating profitable sales. If their partnerships don't meet this goal, then they will move on to a different strategy or different partnership. It is important to be clear about what is bringing your company to the proverbial table.

Motives matter for another reason: the right kind of motives can spark the bright ideas that fuel successful partnerships. Motives help drive the partnership's vision, which we discuss next.

2. The Vision Thing

Research finds that successful, enduring partnerships possess motivating, ambitious visions. AMD and Capital Area Training Foundation, and Manpower and its partners, have the vision to become models to build high-skilled career ladders for individuals living in poor communities. IBM maintains the vision to generate innovations that matter for the company and the world. (Rochlin and Goo-gins, 2004).

Jeff Immelt, CEO of GE, speaks of this type of vision when he talks of the "new economics of scarcity." This involves looking at society's most pressing challenges such as poverty, climate change, opportunities for at-risk youth, health, and others and seeing how business can provide solutions that improve quality of life and create sustainable profits (Rochlin and Googins, 2004).

Nonprofit partners can share in the formation of this vision, as TransFair has helped to shape Green Mountain's vision around fair-trade coffee. Partners become co-conspirators to take a bold and audacious vision and make it a reality. This vision keeps partners focused on the goal and energized to overcome inevitable snafus, setbacks, and crises that emerge along the way.

3. Do the Due Diligence

You should approach a potential partner just as you would a possible joint venture or a new business deal. Due diligence—a careful review of the experience, ability, resources, and trade record of your potential partner—is essential. Is the nonprofit well managed? Is it financially stable? Does it possess a good reputation and brand? Does it have the capabilities to deliver its end of the deal? Are its managers trustworthy, and can you get along with them?

Manpower has a streamlined due diligence process to qualify non-profit partners. Consistent with its competency of institutionalizing best practices and processes, Manpower has developed a partner organization "qualifier," a set of guidelines that local TechReach project managers can use in selecting partner organizations (Center for Corporate Citizenship, 2003).

But the questions given above aren't the only ones that should go into a due diligence process. The due diligence should take a close look at both (1) what capabilities a nonprofit partner can bring to the venture, and (2) what your own company can bring. The box below diagrams the assets that both partners bring to the table. The assets ascend in the potential value that they can provide.

Depending on its motives, a company may start by approaching a nonprofit because its mission is to serve relevant populations and

What assets do nonprofit partners provide to companies?

- Leadership
- Innovation, R&D
- Expertise, local market knowledge, core competencies
- Reputation, credibility
- Mission

What assets do corporate partners provide to nonprofits?

- Leadership
- Innovation, R&D
- Hiring, purchasing, marketing, plant location
- Core competencies, technology transfer, promotion
- Grants, in-kind services, volunteers

because it has a good name in the community. While these are indeed valuable assets, in fact the nonprofit's technical expertise, existing relationships, and ability to innovate often bring the most value to a partnership.

Similarly, nonprofits often start by looking to the company to open its checkbook. However, what often creates the most value are the company's core competencies and ability to transfer its knowledge and technologies to a nonprofit, and its ability to innovate and make decisions that leverage large-scale assets such as hiring and purchasing.

Highest among the assets is each partner's ability to provide leadership that changes the rules of the game and drives new opportunities. See the box on page 189 for a more detailed list of questions to ask about a potential nonprofit partner.

4. Build the Relationship

Companies often learn the hard way that the relationship comes first.

Manpower, for example, found that the partnering process took longer than anticipated. Managers hoped to launch their TechReach partnerships in a three- to four-month timeframe. However, in practice the design and development of the partnerships took at least a year. Manpower learned that the time it takes to launch is related to a gap between the company's and the nonprofit's expectations with respect to time, pace, and language.

For instance, even the most basic terminology created confusion. When Manpower spoke of its "clients," it meant employers. When its potential nonprofit partners spoke of "clients," they meant individuals in the targeted service populations. Also, the language Manpower has used in writing up partnership agreements has sometimes sounded harsh to nonprofit partners. In Manpower's view, the nonprofits' language in these agreements often seemed vague (Center for Corporate Citizenship, 2003).

Kimmo Lipponen, a manager at Nokia, has established well over a dozen win-win partnerships with nonprofit organizations worldwide. Nokia's Make a Connection program builds the ability of youth to have the essential life skills to thrive in a modern, high-tech information society. Its partnership with the International Youth Foundation (IYF) stretches over 20 countries to places as diverse as South Africa, Poland, Korea, Brazil, and Canada. In each locale, Nokia and IYF work with local nonprofits. The vital lesson: successful partnerships require strong relationships.

> We learned that you cannot spend too much time with your partner building relationships and a mutual understanding of each other's core values and goals. Once we have identified a potential partner we spend a lot of time getting to know them and letting them get to know us. Only when we feel like we have a trusting relationship do we actually start to plan our joint venture. It takes a lot of time up front, but creating this kind of social capital pays off by making the partnership more effective, more efficient, and more sustainable. (Lipponen, 2005)

Many managers from companies like State Farm, AMD, TJX, and Union Bank compare the effort to build a successful partnership with that of building a successful marriage. It's important not to rush the courtship period too fast.

The process of building a relationship, as described below, can be very intense:

> Partnering to launch and execute a TechReach program is an intense experience for all parties involved. Partners participate in frequent face-to-face meetings and weekly conference calls

to plan and discuss progress. Issues of power, control, and standards come to the fore as partners learn to work together in service of program delivery. For example, in one local program, the issue of which partner operates as the local "fiscal agent" (the recipient organization of local funding) was a key issue that surfaced in the planning phase. This same partnership had to move through conflict about decision-making authority, requiring partners to confront and discuss honestly assumptions about one another's capacity for accountability. The partners almost walked away from the table several times, a move that would have shut down the project. However, their tenacious commitment to the TechReach mission allowed the partners to stay with the uncomfortable process of working through the issues and eventually formulate agreed upon ways of working together over the life of the project. (Center for Corporate Citizenship, 2003).

5. Build Organizational Capacity

You may find that a potential partner possesses many attributes but also has some deficiencies. Such deficiencies in a nonprofit partner sometimes seem more problematic than they would in a corporate joint venture candidate. Since most nonprofits lack the resources of the private sector, it is not as easy to build operations that can attain the scale in size and customers that corporations need. The nonprofits' key staff and other resources may be stretched.

Therefore, many companies find it is often wise to make the effort to invest in the capacity of its partner. For example, the Kauai Food Bank lacked sufficient experience in production, processing, and a level of quality control that could ensure Grade A products to customers. Its relationship with Marriott exposed deficiencies in refrigeration, in the productivity of the farming operation, and in its quality management systems. The produce wasn't fit for the world-class resort, nor was it available in consistent quantities. To make the partnership work, Marriott realized it would need to provide technical assistance to build the capabilities of the Food Bank to be a high-quality supplier.

Marriott Kauai's executive chef helped advise the Food Bank on

---

Management Tips: Choosing a Partner

1. Does the organization understand your business and, preferably, have staff with relevant business experience?
2. Does the organization have the knowledge, competencies, and relationships to help you achieve your business objectives in underserved markets?
3. Does the organization have credibility (especially with the audiences you want to influence or engage with, both within and outside your company)?
4. Does the organization have experience in business partnerships in underserved markets?
5. Does the organization have sufficient human resource capacity, time, and funding to execute the partnership effectively?
6. Does the organization have a reputation for good management and accountability?

Source: Ford Foundation, 2005.

---

washing, packaging, labeling, and delivering food. The Food Bank acquired a walk-in cooler and a refrigerated truck to keep its produce fresh. But even after the Food Bank improved its growing operations, it remained deficient in the areas of record keeping and marketing. The resort's purchasing agent would not buy produce from the Food Bank because the organization didn't fax him competitive bids listing the week's produce, as did the resort's other wholesalers. The Food Bank had to learn standard food industry business practices in order for customers to consider it a legitimate supplier. So Marriott worked with the Food Bank on fashioning a system to inform customers of its stock. Nearly six months after the program began, the Food Bank made its first sale to Marriott. After Marriott had invested substantial time and energy with the Food Bank, it began to reap the benefits it had hoped for—a high-quality supply of local produce for use in its restaurants (Center for Corporate Citizenship, 2002).

However, learning and growth shouldn't go only one way. Nonprofit partners have much to teach their corporate partners, if managers are willing to listen. As we saw in the Introduction, Self-Help's technical expertise and experience with low-wealth households were invaluable to Fannie Mae as it developed new underwriting guidelines for mortgages.

■ MANAGING THE PARTNERSHIP

Managing a successful partnership takes both skill and effort. There are four steps that your company should follow to successfully manage a partnership:

1. Apply entrepreneurial management strategies
2. Innovate on the existing business model
3. Institutionalize the partnership
4. Know when to end the partnership

1. Apply Entrepreneurial Management Strategies

As goes the adage, necessity is the mother of invention. Great partnerships start with great ideas. This book features great ideas on how to provide scalable financing for affordable housing, build career ladders in information technology for underserved populations, create a profitable consumer base in communities with household incomes well below the median, develop minority- and women-owned businesses that serve as reliable suppliers, build safer homes that reduce costs to the insured and the insurer, and test new, innovative products by serving community needs.

However, once you have a great idea, you shouldn't rush to build a rigid operational plan. Be aware that win-win partnerships are often designed specifically to test new ideas and find new ways to get things done. As such, these partnerships challenge existing orthodoxies. Sometimes they may even outright break the rules of the way the bureaucracy works in your company.

It's often better to think of a win-win partnership as an entrepreneurial start-up fueled by a great and exciting idea. Many companies find that allowing the terms and direction of the partnership to remain a little fuzzy is valuable. First, there is the "elephant" problem. Dealing with a complex and unfamiliar system can seem like the parable of the blind men and the elephant. No partner sees the entire system, market, or set of issues. If you set rigid goals at the beginning, you do so with incomplete knowledge of the whole system, the scope of problems, and the possible solutions. It takes time, communication, learning, and some trial and error to understand the market and its opportunities and risks. In this way, partners can experiment, try new approaches, and change course if necessary. This approach also allows even better ideas to emerge that deliver higher payoffs (Manga and Shah, 2005).

Second, often the most creative breakthroughs come laterally, and not with the problems you start with. For example, Manpower got involved with the Department of Labor's One-Stop program to provide training. But the company found that Manpower could actually *sell* its own training to the One-Stop program! Working to rigid goals and specifications from the outset limits your ability to take full advantage of the partnership. When you remain open, unexpected opportunities open up.

For example, State Farm established a partnership with Neighborhood Housing Services (NHS), a nonprofit urban revitalization advocacy group, in 1978. At first, the partnership was designed as an initiative to minimize the risk associated with potential claims of discriminatory behavior in low-income communities. State Farm would work with NHS to support community development and address any perceived or real concerns that the company was engaged in discriminatory practices.

However, by working together in a flexible, entrepreneurial fashion, both partners discovered an opportunity to change and improve the purpose and goals of the partnership. The partnership grew to find ways to provide "affordable and appropriate insurance products in low-income communities" (Manga and Shah, 2005, p. 6).

Thom Branch, Senior Vice President and Manager, Nix Alliance for Union Bank of California, has learned that it is not essential for successful partnerships to establish rigid objectives and performance measures at their inception. Rather, it is important to be what he calls "directionally correct." Research conducted by Julie Manga and Sapna Shah finds that it is important for partners to seek to establish a common, bold, and energizing vision for their work, and then treat their venture like an incubating start-up (Manga and Shah, 2005, p. 13).

In this regard, Manga and Shah find that successful, sustainable partnerships proceed through stages of maturity similar to an entre-preneurial startup: entrepreneurial stage, development stage, and mature stage. In the entrepreneurial stage, the partners go through a "dating period" that builds confidence and establishes the opportuni-ties for their work. In the development stage, partners move to estab-lish more formal timetables and plans. In the mature stage, partners assess the impact and success of their work. This phase determines whether there is an opportunity to expand the scale and scope of the work, or to move in an alternative direction (Manga and Shah, 2005, p. 26).

2. Innovate on the Existing Business Model

One of the five key success factors discussed throughout this book is "Adapt business model to community realities." In successful part-nerships, both partners innovate on their existing business models and make them more appropriate both for addressing community realities and also for working with each other. This process can be challenging at times. Differences in business models and assump-tions may make each partner feel that the other simply doesn't understand the issues or isn't really committed. But win-win part-ners supply enough benefit to each other that they can maintain the commitment to the partnership and use the differences to drive innovation on the business model. As we saw previously, TransFair helped Green Mountain to innovate on its purchasing and sales models. Fannie Mae innovated the way that it underwrote its mort-gage product with the assistance of Self-Help. And State Farm adapted its sales and development process to expand its market.

3. Institutionalize the Partnership

In their research on enduring partnerships, Manga and Shah found that a key factor enabling a partnership to survive and thrive in the face of inevitable setbacks is the "degree to which it is institutional-ized or integrated into the structure and culture of the participating organizations" (Manga and Shah, 2005, p. 14). The key factors that help to institutionalize a partnership are as follows:

Establish Multiple Points of Contact. The sustainability of a partnership over time hinges on whether relationships can broaden and "spill into several different arenas within each organization." For example, the partnership between State Farm and NHS started with individuals and departments involved in charitable giving and regulation management. It grew to involve product and market development and became incorporated into the employee volunteer program. The development of the National Insurance Task Force became a forum for wider collaboration between managers from the two organizations plus additional insurance companies (p. 17).

Ensure Internal Organizational Support. Without broader organizational commitment and support, the risk increases that partnerships will eventually dissipate. Partnerships need the active blessing of senior executives, who should bring rhetoric into reality by assigning appropriate staff and resources to the effort. This includes providing clear objectives and incentives (such as through the performance review) for managers involved.

At the start of a partnership, however, many managers inside both organizations may view the partnership with skepticism. Therefore, Manga and Shah find that it is critical for partnerships to establish a "torchbearer"—usually a relatively senior manager or an individual who is greatly respected. The torchbearer becomes not only the internal leader of the partnership but also its advocate who builds internal support. Thom Branch, a senior executive with extensive line experience, plays the role of torchbearer for Union Bank's partnership with Operation Hope (pp. 18–19).

Align the Partners' Operating Assumptions. Experience and inertia will lead partners to rely on their standard operating procedures and usual ways of doing business. But successful partnerships typically seek to break the mold. Early on, it is essential for partners to become aligned in their understanding of the marketplace, its needs, its opportunities, its risks, and the options for action.

For example, NHS spent "significant time undoing the assumptions of some insurance agents and underwriters, including those at State Farm" (p. 20). Many of the underwriters were unfamiliar with the risks and opportunities in underserved neighborhoods and therefore perceived them as risky ventures. Many agents assumed that residents would take on excessive insurance and then damage their own property to seek a financial windfall. Manga and Shah write:

> To counteract that assumption NHS representatives took agents and underwriters into these neighborhoods and introduced them to residents; it became clear these people were not inclined to burn down their own homes. (pp. 19–20)

Phase in Measurement. The adage goes that what gets measured, gets managed. However, experienced partners warn others not to rush to build detailed and formalized measurement processes too soon. Manga and Shah find that measurement matures along with the partners. At the outset, it is important to set broad measures that signal whether the partnership seems on the right track. Measuring too rigidly at this stage may inhibit the ability of a partnership to adapt to new opportunities and circumstances. Once the direction of the partnership appears set, then the participating organizations should work to capture a wide variety of data points that determine both outcomes and impacts (pp. 26–27).

4. Know When to End the Partnership

Successful partnerships can last a long time. If both partners continue to derive value, meet goals, and deliver win-win results, then like other successful ventures there should be no move to prematurely exit the relationship.

However, some managers may feel anxious that partnerships with nonprofits will be challenging to launch and even more difficult to end. They may be familiar with relationships where nonprofits come to rely on annual corporate gifts in cash or in kind. Ending this type of relationship can be painful for both sides.

But win-win partnerships with nonprofits need not endure in perpetuity. If you think about the kind of partnership that you would form with another for-profit company, the agreement would typically specify the terms of engagement, the partnership's scope, expected timing of key results, and an estimated end date. At that time, the partners would make a decision whether or not to extend the relationship, but generally only in the context of establishing new goals and objectives.

The same applies for win-win partnerships with nonprofits. The relationship is not meant to be one of munificence. Both partners will likely possess an interest in defining a beginning and end point. Making sure to specify this up front will not only facilitate project management but also minimize difficult issues at the end of the project's duration.

There are several important components to ending a partnership well. The first is to have clear criteria and a specified process for ending the partnership. Both sides should understand (1) why the other is in the partnership, and (2) what criteria each partner will use to decide to end its participation in the partnership. If, for example, the partnership is focused on building profitable sales, then both sides should have an understanding of what level of sales increase is needed to keep the partnership going.

A second important component is agreement beforehand about ownership of the tangible and intangible assets of the partnership. Who owns the intellectual capital—the knowledge and insights? If there are co-branded products, what happens to them when the partnership ends? What about the relationships with funders and customers?

Third, it is useful to think through an exit strategy that ensures that neither partner is unduly burdened when the partnership ends. Can the work of the partnership continue in some other form? Are there potential new partners who could take over some of the work or provide some funding? Can the nonprofit help to guarantee that the community still sees the corporation as a good neighbor even when it ends the partnership? Working to ensure that the partnership ends well can be an important tool for ensuring that future partnerships can be started well.

PUTTING IT ALL TOGETHER: CASE STUDY

This chapter has shown that managing successful partnerships takes effort but produces rewards. We've outlined critical success factors that make partnerships work. Throughout the book, we have illustrated how companies use partnerships to compete in underserved markets. This case study of how TJX and Morgan Memorial Goodwill Industries of Boston have been able to build and maintain their partnership draws together and illustrates the points we have discussed.

The TJX Companies, Inc., operates eight divisions: T.J. Maxx, Marshalls, HomeGoods, A.J. Wright, and Bob's Stores in the United States; Winners and HomeSense in Canada; and T.K. Maxx in Europe. The company's target customer is a middle- to upper-middle-income shopper who is fashion and value conscious and fits the same profile as a department store shopper. TJX's mission is to deliver a rapidly changing assortment of quality, brand-name merchandise at prices that are always 20 to 60 percent lower than department and specialty store regular prices. In 2002, the TJX Companies' retail sales reached $12 billion, with a total of 1,843 stores and 4,000 associates. Morgan Memorial Goodwill Industries' mission is to provide exemplary job training and related services to help individuals with disabilities and other barriers to self-sufficiency to achieve independence and dignity through work (Center for Corporate Citizenship, 2004c; this case discussion draws extensively from the research of Julie Manga and Sapna Shah at the Center for Corporate Citizenship at Boston College).

■ STARTING THE PARTNERSHIP

1. Know Yourself—Motives Matter

The partnership, created in 1997 when then-president Bill Clinton challenged companies to create jobs to support his welfare-to-work initiative, is an innovative collaboration of two off-price retail operations.

TJX's CEO felt the company could rise to the challenge and expected to secure an untapped workforce of loyal, productive individuals during a time of dynamic economic growth. For its part, Goodwill had launched an ambitious initiative to train and place welfare recipients into new job opportunities.

Since TJX was having a difficult time hiring entry-level workers, former welfare recipients who had participated in a carefully designed program fit an important business need for new, well-trained employees. Joining forces to develop a welfare-to-work program made good business sense for both TJX and Goodwill. For its part, Goodwill saw the partnership with TJX as an opportunity to expand its reputation and the organization's ability to serve its clientele (Center for Corporate Citizenship, 2004c).

2. The Vision Thing

TJX's CEO made the bold commitment to hire 5,000 former welfare recipients. His vision, while motivating, also made clear the need to find a capable partner.

3. Do the Due Diligence

TJX is in the retail apparel business, not the welfare-to-work business. It needed to find a capable partner that would combine effective skills and competencies as well as a reputation that would reinforce the credibility of TJX's intentions.

> Goodwill was an ideal partner because of its 100-year experience in providing job and vocational training for people with disabilities and operating retail stores that resell clothing and household goods. Unlike some of the other workforce development agencies in the area, Goodwill had many years of experience in finding employment for people with physical, mental, and other disabilities—the individuals considered the most difficult to place. Thus, the organization was already well positioned to deal with the types of barriers that welfare recipients often face in securing employment. (Center for Corporate Citizenship, 2004c, p. 2)

4. Build the Relationship and
5. Build Organizational Capacity

Prospects for a successful partnership were enhanced by multiple connections between the organizations—including membership on a regional business advisory group. Also, for years TJX had been the largest contributor to Goodwill's annual clothing drive. A manager from Goodwill spent an 18 month "dating period" interviewing TJX employees and becoming familiar with various aspects of the business—from hiring to pay structures. The effort paid off and now some of the best champions are the TJX store managers most skeptical at the start. (Manga and Shah, 2005, p. 15)

■ MANAGING THE PARTNERSHIP

1. Apply Entrepreneurial Management Strategies

Goodwill and TJX began developing their pilot program, which they called the First Step. The program provided three weeks of classroom training, a three- to five-week paid internship, and a full year of case management for participants to support their transition to work.

In 2001, members of the Boston-area Latina population had begun to approach Goodwill because of additional obstacles they were facing, not only as welfare recipients with limited education, but also because of language barriers and the lack of information they were receiving about welfare reform. In 2002, Goodwill and TJX decided to expand the First Step program to include this population, and Goodwill incorporated bilingual job training and case management into the program and ran either English-based or Spanish-based cycles, based on the participants' needs. (Center for Corporate Citizenship, 2004c, p. 6)

2. Innovate on the Existing Business Model

The program received funding from the federal welfare-to-work program. Requirements for funding mandated that program graduates be hired into full-time positions.

This requirement was a major consideration, since TJX stores are traditionally supported by a part-time workforce. TJX accommodated this requirement so that the company could participate in offering the First Step program. (Center for Corporate Citizenship, 2004c, p. 4)

3. Institutionalize the Partnership

Goodwill and TJX set up two elements that became cornerstones of their successful partnership: an advisory committee, and orientation sessions for the TJX store managers who were going to be involved with the program. The advisory committee included representatives from Goodwill program and retail staff, TJX executives, store managers, human resource representatives, managers, and district managers—in other words, all First Step program stakeholders. The 15 to 18 committee members met quarterly to review program performance and oversee program management. This team worked to strategically advise as well as manage the implementation of the program and the partnership as a whole. (Center for Corporate Citizenship, 2004c, p. 4)

TJX's Patrick Flavin, manager of government programs, was put in charge of the partnership. To ensure a proper transition, Flavin for four months shadowed his predecessor, who was transferring responsibility for the partnership.

Other supportive infrastructure comes in the form of an employer liaison position, an agent of transition who facilitates the participants' smooth entry into the workforce. When Goodwill's manager for the partnership left the organization, those integral to the partnership from both organizations met to review the status, revise the communications strategy, and review the five year evaluation and planning process. These actions helped re-engage some and introduce others to the partnership. To further institutionalize the venture with TJX, Flavin is creating a manual that will document program protocols, details, and technicalities. Goodwill has also documented many of the best practices from the partnership and implemented them in other parts of its operation. TJX and Goodwill also plan to develop a "how-to" book for retailers at the state and national levels. (Manga and Shah, 2005, p. 15)

As of 2003, the program had maintained an entered-employment rate of over 90 percent and a retention rate of 80 percent of participants who worked for three months or more. TJX reported that the employees hired by TJX from the First Step program demonstrated a 20 to 30 percent better retention rate than traditional hires.

4. Know When to End the Partnership

The partnership between TJX and Goodwill is still going strong. This is in part due to the fact that both partners have clear measures for understanding how the partnership contributes to their bottom lines. Having clear measures for success lets both parties know whether or not continuing to invest time and energy makes sense. As of 2005, the First Step program is now in its eighth year of operation because it makes good business sense for both partners to continue. As CEO Ted English of TJX notes,

> We have had a very high retention rate for sales associates hired through Goodwill. This is a direct result of our great, long-standing partnership.

And Goodwill is satisfied with the partnership because it enables them to place their clients in jobs—which is a core program goal (Goodwill, 2005).

■ CONCLUSION ■

To compete in underserved markets, whether tapping new markets, recruiting and retaining a qualified workforce, increasing value in the supply chain, or leveraging innovation and R&D, *the right partnership is everything*. Win-win partnerships are a key component of all five success factors for creating value in underserved markets. They are more and more part of business as usual. And they are particularly deserving of management attention because they are challenging to do well.

Successful partnerships share common features. The partners have shared goals and objectives. The partnership is not a "work for hire," in which one partner is simply buying services from the other. There is a division of labor and resources, as well as mutual expectations to produce products and services for all partners and for the community. Win-win partnerships typically require planning and explicit agreements on roles and responsibilities, particularly as they grow in scale and the number of people involved.

■ STARTING THE PARTNERSHIP

When starting the partnership, it is important to begin by (1) understanding the complex set of motivations that drive your own organization, and (2) communicating them to your partner. Ask the same in return. It is important to invest time up front to get to know a potential partner before launching a formal initiative. The better you each understand the other's motives, the more creativity you can jointly develop in finding new ways to generate value.

Part of the time you invest up front should be used to do a due diligence review. Explore the background, history, assets, and liabilities of your potential partner, in the same way as you would any other potential joint venture. It is worthwhile spending time to explore the unique assets and capabilities that both your company and your potential nonprofit partner can bring to the table. Go beyond the basics (e.g., money for corporate partners, credibility in underserved communities for the nonprofit) to understand the high-value assets each partner can contribute. It is also important to look for potential pitfalls and to determine how best to protect against them.

In launching the partnership, it is useful to develop as concrete a vision statement as possible. How will both partners be better off? What does success look like? The vision statement can be used to motivate commitment from all participants and also to ensure that everyone's vision of success is aligned.

In the early stages of the partnership, it may be necessary to build organizational capacity, either in your own organization or in your partner's. Early-stage capacity building can pay off in significant ways later on in the partnership. Building capabilities is not a one-way street. Companies that are open to learning from their nonprofit partners often find creative, innovative solutions that generate opportunities.

■ MANAGING THE PARTNERSHIP

Like all business activities, partnerships require focused management. Because many partnerships seek to generate innovation, focused management does not necessarily imply a rigid management plan. Getting too rigid too soon will mean that the team may miss out on the opportunity to explore and test interesting options that arise in the course of developing the partnership. It is better to manage the partnership more like an entrepreneurial start-up and less like an assembly line. The partnership will then be better able to modify and adapt existing business models to better fit the opportunities and circumstances of underserved markets.

If they are successful, win-win partnerships grow over time and shift from being dependent on the relationship between two key managers, one in each organization, to being institutionalized across both organizations, involving many individuals and multiple points of contact. Managers will need to focus on developing broad internal organizational support and aligning the partners' operating assumptions as the partnership continues over time.

Finally, it is important to know when to stop. Partnerships, like all other business activities, need benchmarks for continuing—and ending. It is helpful to clarify the ownership of assets while the partnership is doing well, rather than when it is time to shut down. It also is helpful to commit to a process for ending that ensures that each partner comes out "whole" at the end of the relationship, and willing to enter into another partnership in the future.

For additional case studies and further details, see the following websites:

Account Ability: www.conversations-with-disbelievers.net
The Center for Corporate Citizenship at Boston College: www.bcccc.net
Win-Win Partners: www.winwinpartner.com
World Business Council for Sustainable Development: www.wbcsd.com

6

CREATING VALUE FOR BUSINESS AND COMMUNITY

Businesses can create value for themselves and for communities by tapping opportunities in underserved markets. They can develop profitable new sales, improve brand and reputation, meet their workforce needs, find new suppliers, and accelerate product and process innovation. They can enable consumers in underserved communities to get access to a broader range of products at better prices. They can establish opportunities for individuals in underserved communities to obtain good-paying jobs and find a career path. They can open up avenues for increased sales by businesses located in these communities. They also can create methods for members of underserved communities to influence and improve the design of products and the mix of merchandise offered in their communities.

But there are also real possibilities for problems if these activities are not done well. Companies can find that community opposition stalls their projects. They can find that they aren't getting good recruits, or that the recruits are turning over quickly, or that the recruits aren't able to advance within the company. They can find that suppliers from underserved communities aren't meeting requirements for quality, timeliness, and financial stability. They can find that their approaches to product innovation aren't in fact leading to new products that achieve high levels of sales in underserved communities.

How can you ensure that your company creates value for itself and for underserved communities? As we noted in the Introduction, it comes down to one key fact: *a win-win relationship is everything*. Creating a win-win relationship between company and community is critical for success in these markets. Without such a relationship, a corporation essentially re-creates colonialism. It takes much of value from these communities and delivers little of value in return. This kind of relationship is innately unstable. Examples throughout this book have illustrated the kinds of problems that occur when community residents feel that the relationship is not win-win.

But how do you create a win-win relationship? By always keeping in mind the five success strategies that enable companies to create value for both themselves and underserved communities:

1. Mine and translate local market information.
2. Adapt business model to community realities.
3. Change internal incentives and challenge cultural assumptions.
4. Create partnerships and strategic alliances.
5. Improve the enabling environment.

These five strategies generate specific approaches to develop mutually beneficial relationships. Each factor can be adapted to provide guidance in four business disciplines: sales and marketing, human resources, purchasing, and process and product development. Let's consider how the first success strategy—mine and translate local market information—is adapted from business discipline to business discipline, always being driven by the ways that the market and environment in underserved communities differ from those in mainstream communities.

For *sales and marketing*, underserved markets can pose challenges because (1) underserved markets are more heterogeneous than mainstream markets, and (2) standard analytic techniques developed for mainstream markets can lead to inaccurate or misleading conclusions when applied to underserved markets. Accordingly, "mine and translate local market information" for sales and marketing requires using the skills and resources of other organizations that have developed specialized information on these communities, and developing "learning laboratories"—processes for improving your company's ability to identify and analyze data that will accurately predict sales and market behavior. Fannie Mae faced this challenge when it sought to increase its purchases of loans from members of the underserved community. Through its partnership with Self-Help, it was able to obtain specialized information in order to customize existing products and sell them profitably in underserved markets. This also enabled it to help increase the provision of more affordable mortgages to consumers in underserved communities.

For *human resources*, underserved markets can be challenging because the social networks connecting jobseekers to the company are likely to be much weaker in underserved markets than in mainstream markets. In response, the company must build new social networks and career pathways, and create relationships with important institutions in the underserved community. Through these approaches, the company can establish the social networks needed to efficiently connect jobseekers with the company. DreamWorks collaborated with Workplace Hollywood to create settings in which union members employed in the production side of the movie business taught classes to youths from underserved communities interested in obtaining employment in production jobs. The classes promoted the kinds of social networks needed for the youths to be matched up effectively with jobs in the industry.

Turning to *purchasing*, one of the key challenges is that existing business networks don't do a good job of helping companies to find vendors from underserved communities that meet their requirements. This is a variation of the problem that businesses confront in finding employees from underserved neighborhoods. The business network connecting vendors and potential customers is weak or nonexistent. Without such a network, it is harder for businesses to find vendors and then to determine their quality and reliability.

One strategy to overcome the lack of a business network between companies and vendors is to use purchasing brokers to identify appropriate vendors in underserved markets and build productive relationships. The National Minority Supplier Development Organization is a good example. With its 3,500 corporate members, all of whom are looking for minority-owned suppliers, and its database of

15,000 certified minority-owned suppliers, it is an entire network unto itself.

Another strategy for overcoming the lack of a business network is for the company to create settings that help suppliers develop relationships with its managers and the managers of its first-tier suppliers. For example, DaimlerChrysler's Automotive Matchmaker conferences from 2000 to 2005 have generated more than $500 million in new business for minority-owned business enterprises (MBEs) by enabling Chrysler team members, customers, and a wide range of suppliers to meet and learn about each other's requirements, goods, and services.

Finally, with *process and product development,* a key challenge is that the managers who run the product development process often have a much lower level of personal familiarity with underserved markets than with more mainstream markets. The process of generating new ideas, and choosing which ideas to develop into products, depends in part on managers' intuition about which products are likely to be attractive to customers. If the business managers don't have personal experience and understanding of these markets, their intuition is likely not to be as good.

To address this challenge, companies re-engineer their community engagement processes to develop information that's useful for innovation. CEMEX is a good example. Instead of using standard approaches to gathering and analyzing data for product development, it sent managers to live in the underserved communities to understand how individuals already planned and financed their "do-it-yourself" projects. Such deep engagement with the communities facilitated the development of an entirely new approach to selling cement to low-income households.

Companies also follow collaborative approaches to developing information that is useful for innovation. Sharing the costs brings down the cost per company to a manageable level. Not surprisingly, this approach works best when companies that are not competitors want to develop a better understanding of the same market segment. The Base of the Pyramid project is one such example. Its corporate members are SC Johnson, DuPont, and Hewlett-Packard—companies whose product lines don't overlap much, if at all.

As this discussion shows, the success factor "mine and translate local market information" is adapted from business discipline to business discipline according to specific challenges in underserved markets. We could do a similar analysis with the other four success factors. For each factor, we could develop a similar list of challenges and successful solutions.

Although there are many challenges in entering underserved markets, the typical solution requires a company to enhance and adapt what it is already doing, not to entirely reinvent itself. Entering underserved markets requires that the company make strategic adjustments, not become an entirely new company.

Strategies for implementing the success factors often involve creating partnerships and alliances. This is an important approach in many situations. As the examples throughout this book demonstrate, partnerships can range from one-to-one partnerships (e.g., between Marriott and the Kauai Food Bank) to business alliances (e.g., Metropolis 2020) to complex multi-sector collaborations (e.g., the National Insurance Task Force). Partnerships and alliances are so important for success in entering underserved markets that we have devoted an entire chapter to the techniques and tools for creating and managing them (see Chapter 5).

All of the success factors and strategies in this book show you how to engage with underserved communities in ways that create a win-win relationship for your business and community alike. Your business can gain profitable sales, attract a workforce, find suppliers, and develop new products and processes, all of which is good. But there is another deeper and more profound reason for your business to engage with underserved communities: the pressing need for business to help build a world that works for all.

Almost all the growth in population over the next fifty years will occur in underserved communities. They will grow at very significant rates, adding millions of people a year, mostly in cities in the developing world. The best current projections suggest that underserved communities in developing countries will need to build the equivalent of a city of more than one million people each week for the next 45 years. The growing population will need jobs, homes, infrastructure, and most important, hope. Businesses can be a critical source of all of these (Cohen, 2005).

Business, with its vast resources and know-how, can be an important contributor in creating a world in which these individuals can meet their basic needs. If business steps up to the challenge, it can play a crucial role in opening up a world of opportunity rather than despair. If, instead, business turns aside from engaging with underserved communities, it is likely that children across the globe will grow up knowing a world in which there are only islands of wealth in a sea of poverty. Such a world would be filled with despair and violence. Such a world would not be welcoming for our children, or our children's children. Business can help make the difference. This book provides the tools that you need both to create profitable engagement with underserved communities and also to help transform the world so that it can promise a decent livelihood and a future of hope for all.

Useful Web Resources

www.bcccc.net
The Center for Corporate Citizenship at Boston College is a corporate membership–based research organization. It works with global corporations to help them define, plan, and implement their corporate citizenship. Its goal is to help business leverage its social, economic, and human assets to ensure both its success and a more just and sustainable world. For 20 years the Center for Corporate Citizenship has provided research, executive education, and conferences to help its members achieve performance excellence in corporate citizenship.

www.bsr.org
Business for Social Responsibility (BSR) is a global organization that helps member companies achieve success in ways that respect ethical values, people, communities, and the environment. BSR provides information, tools, training, and advisory services to make corporate social responsibility an integral part of business operations and strategies. A nonprofit organization, BSR promotes cross-sector collaboration and contributes to global efforts to advance the field of corporate social responsibility.

www.codesofconduct.org
This Web site provides a useful resource for those interested in the full text of various codes of conduct and information about their provisions, sponsors, and effects on business practices.

(continued)

www.conversations-with-disbelievers.net
The Conversations with Disbelievers Web site brings together quantitative evidence that demonstrates that addressing social challenges can help businesses improve their financial bottom lines. It provides convincing data in the form of case studies and special reports, as well as the latest headline news from around the world.

www.dreamit-doit.com
The goal of the "Dream It. Do It." campaign is to help young adults find careers that they can be passionate about in one of manufacturing's many exciting sectors. The "Dream It. Do It." campaign was developed by the National Association of Manufacturers (NAM) and the Manufacturing Institute, its research and education affiliate. NAM is the largest industrial trade association in the United States, representing small and large manufacturers in every industrial sector and in all 50 states. For more information about the NAM, visit www.nam.org.

www.iblf.org
The International Business Leaders Forum is an international UK-based nonprofit organization set up in 1990 by HRH the Prince of Wales and a group of chief executives of international companies in response to the emerging challenges of economic growth and change in the global economy. Its mission is to promote responsible business leadership and partnerships for social, economic, and environmentally sustainable international development, particularly in new and emerging market economies.

www.ism.ws
Founded in 1915, the Institute for Supply Management (ISM) is the largest supply management association in the world, as well as one of the most respected. ISM's mission is to lead the supply management profession through its standards of excellence, research, promotional activities, and education. ISM's membership base includes more than 40,000 supply management professionals with a network of domestic and international affiliated associations. ISM is a not-for-profit association that provides opportunities for the promotion of the profession and the expansion of professional skills and knowledge.

www.jff.org
A Boston-based, national nonprofit research, consulting, and advocacy organization, JFF works to strengthen society by creating educational and economic opportunity for those who need it most. JFF accelerates opportunities for people to advance in education and careers through research, analysis, and policy development; practical, on-the-ground projects; and advocacy, communications, and peer learning.

(continued)

www.nextbillion.net
NextBillion.net, launched in May 2005, is a Web site sponsored by the World Resources Institute. It is both a knowledge repository and a space for discussion and networking among those with an interest in the "next billion"—the base of the pyramid (BOP)—as participants in healthy economies, and the next billion in profits earned by businesses, from multinational to microenterprises, that sell to underserved markets.

www.nmsdcus.org
The National Minority Supplier Development Council (NMSDC) was chartered in 1972 to increase procurement and business opportunities for minority businesses of all sizes. The NMSDC, headquartered in New York, certifies and matches more than 15,000 minority-owned businesses with member corporations (exceeding 3,500) that want to purchase goods and services.

www.sa-intl.org
SAI is an international nonprofit human rights organization dedicated to the ethical treatment of workers around the world. SAI's social standard, called SA8000, functions as a highly effective and expedient system for delivering improved social performance to businesses and their supply chain facilities. SAI convenes key stakeholders to build consensus-based ethical workplace standards, accredits qualified organizations to verify compliance with these standards, and promotes the understanding and implementation of social performance standards worldwide.

www.transfairusa.org
TransFair USA, a nonprofit organization, is one of 19 members of the Fairtrade Labeling Organizations International (FLO), and the only third-party certifier of Fair Trade products in the United States. It audits transactions between U.S. companies offering Fair Trade Certified products and the international suppliers from whom they source, in order to guarantee that the farmers and farm workers behind Fair Trade Certified goods were paid a fair, above-market price.

www.wbcsd.org
The World Business Council for Sustainable Development (WBCSD) is a coalition of 180 international companies united by a shared commitment to sustainable development via economic growth, ecological balance, and social progress. Its members are drawn from more than 35 countries and 20 major industrial sectors. Its mission is to provide business leadership as a catalyst for change toward sustainable development and to promote the role of eco-efficiency, innovation, and corporate social responsibility.

(continued)

www.winwinpartner.com
Win-Win Partners is an online clearinghouse of information on companies and organizations that achieve competitive advantage through community investment. It is a good resource for identifying partners, and includes a library of reports and information about strategies relevant to reaching underserved markets.

www.workforceadvantage.org
WorkforceAdvantage.org identifies and documents the most innovative practices for enhancing employment opportunities for entry-level and low-skilled workers in the nation's inner cities. It offers case examples and other helping resources. It is a joint initiative of Jobs for the Future and the Initiative for a Competitive Inner City.

www.wri.org
The World Resources Institute is an environmental think tank that goes beyond research to create practical ways to protect the earth and improve people's lives. WRI provides objective information and practical proposals for policy and institutional change that will foster environmentally sound, socially equitable development.

❏ REFERENCES

Introduction: Finding the Opportunities

CEMEX. 2005. Building a better society. August 25. www.cemex.com/cc/cc_cc.asp.

Center for Corporate Citizenship at Boston College. 2003. In practice: ManPower case study. February.

First Data. 2004. Banks seek to cash in on money wiring. June 28. www.firstdata.com/news_article.jsp?nID = 1895.

Ford Foundation. 2005. Part of the solution: Leveraging business and markets for low-income people.

Grunewald, Michael. 1999. Harlem finally rides the economy's 'A' train: As crime falls, a retail boom arrives. *Washington Post,* May 5: A01.

Sandoval, Ricardo. 2005. Block by block: How one of the world's largest companies builds loyalty among Mexico's poor. *Stanford Social Innovation Review* (Summer).

Thomas, Greg. 2003. Pataki's man in Harlem: How Randy Daniels helped put chain stores and market prices uptown. *Village Voice,* February 4.

Vision. 2005. Client stories. August 25. www.vision.com/clients/client_stories/cemex_pat.html5.

WinWinPartner.com. 2005. November 5. www.winwinpartner.com/Developing%20Untapped%20Markets/ssPathmark.html.

Chapter 1: Tapping New Markets

Business in the Community. 2005. Home Group Ltd.—"North Benwell Management Initiative." November 18. www.bitc.org.uk/resources/case _studies/home_group_ltd.html.

Chua, Amy. 2004. *World on fire: How exporting free market democracy breeds ethnic hatred and global instability.* New York: Anchor Books, 2004.

Cisco Systems. 2005. About the Networking Academy. November 18. www .cisco.com/web/learning/netacad/academy/About.html.

Committee to Encourage Corporate Philanthropy. 2005. Annual Award Presentation, February 28.

Dunn, Debra, and Keith Yamashita. 2003. Microcapitalism and the megacorporation. *Harvard Business Review,* August: 46–54.

Fannie Mae. 2003. December 31. www.fanniemae.com/index.jhtml.

Ford Foundation. 2005. Part of the solution: Leveraging business and markets for low-income people.

Green, Dawne. 2004. Loss prevention partnerships program: Expanding across the network. Bright Ideas, Spring. Neighborhood Reinvestment Corporation. www.nw.org/network/homeframex.asp?searchfor=12.

Hart, Stuart, and Clayton Christensen. 2002. The great leap. *MIT Sloan Management Review* (Fall).

Humphreys, Jeffrey. 2004. The multicultural economy 2004: America's minority buying power. Selig Center for Economic Growth, University of Georgia. Third Quarter.

Initiative for a Competitive Inner City. 2002. The changing models of inner city grocery retailing.

Initiative for a Competitive Inner City. 2004. April 25. www.icic.org/ research/research_facts.asp.

Initiative for a Competitive Inner City. 2005. Seven years of the Inner City 100. www.icic.org.

Kahane, Michele. 2004. Presentation to Council on Foundations Annual Conference. April 27.

Lobenhofer, Jennifer S., Caryn Bredenkamp, and Michael A. Stegman. 2003. Standard Bank of South Africa's E plan: Harnessing ATM technology to expand banking services. Center for Community Capitalism, University of North Carolina at Chapel Hill. www.kenan-flagler.unc.edu/assets/ documents/CC_Standard_Bank_of_South_Africa_E-Plan.pdf.

Masterson, Sheila. 2001. Interview regarding Shaw's Supermarket. June 13.

National Minority Supplier Development Council. 2005. Annual report 2003. August 1. www.nmsdcus.org/infocenter/NMSDC.Annual_Rpt .2003.pdf.

Partridge, Brooke. 2003. Presentation to Ford Foundation grantee convening. June 2.

Pittman, Todd. 2004a. NeighborWorks Insurance Alliance. *Bright Ideas* (Spring). Neighborhood Reinvestment Corporation. www.nw.org/network/homeframex.asp?searchfor=12.

Pittman, Todd. 2004b. Conversation about expansion of loss prevention partnerships. April 13.

Prahalad, C.K., 2004. Emerging global economic system: The driving forces. Presentation at WRI Sustainable Enterprise Summit, March 17–18. http://summit.wri.org/2004_content_ppts.cfm.

Prahalad, C.K., and Allen Hammond. 2004. Serving the poor profitably. World Resources Institute. April 25. www.digitaldividend.org/pdf/serving_profitably.pdf.

Prahalad, C.K., and Stuart L. Hart. 2002. The fortune at the bottom of the pyramid. *Strategy + Business* 26 (First Quarter).

Rochlin, Steven, and Janet Boguslaw. 2001. Business and community development: Aligning corporate performance with community economic development to achieve win-win impacts. Center for Corporate Citizenship at Boston College.

Social Compact. 2004. District of Columbia neighborhood market drill down. March 28. www.socialcompact.org/pdfs/pdf_district_of_columbia_consolidated_report.pdf.

Social Compact. 2005. Alternative data sources. November 18. www.socialcompact.org/market.htm.

Standard Bank. 2004. Sustainability report 2004. www.standardbank.co.za/site/investor/sr_2004/sustainabilityreportoverview.htm.

Weiser, John, and Simon Zadek. 2000. *Conversations with disbelievers: Persuading companies to address social challenges.* New York: Ford Foundation.

WinWinPartner.com. 2004. February 20. www.winwinpartner.com/Developing%20Untapped%20Markets/ssCitigroup.html.

Women's World Banking. 2005. Women's World Banking vision and key messages. September 12. www.swwb.org/English/1000/affiliates/vision_statement_of_wwb_affiliate_leaders.htm.

Working Today. 2004. Presentation to Ford Foundation PRI meeting. October 1.

Yago, Glenn, and Aaron Pankratz. 2004. The minority business challenge: Democratizing capital for emerging domestic markets. Milken Institute. September 25.

Chapter 2: Recruiting and Retaining a Qualified Workforce

Alexander, Keith L. 2000. Unlikely leaders. *Emerge* 11 (8).

American Association of Engineering Societies. 2002. Public Policy Statement. www.aaes.org/public-policy/8-26-02.asp.

Bison.com. 2005. Marriott named one of the 100 best companies for working mothers. June 8. www.bison1.com/press/pr9-24-02marriott.html.

Caldwell, Melinda. 2001. Recruitment—An essential component of your marketing strategy. *Structural Building Components Magazine* (August).

Center for Corporate Citizenship at Boston College. 2001. Business and community development: Aligning corporate performance with community economic development to achieve win-win impacts.

Center for Corporate Citizenship at Boston College. 2004. The state of corporate citizenship in the U.S. December.

Corporate Voices for Working Families. 2005. Our work. November 13. www.cvworkingfamilies.org/facts/facts.shtml.

Cox, Taylor H., and Ruby L. Beale. 1997. *Developing competency to manage diversity*. San Francisco, CA: Berrett-Koehler.

CSR Europe. 2005. Lifelong learning at the heart of an entrepreneurial and inclusive Europe. November 18. http://64.233.161.104/search?q=cache:95zChlYePjoJ:www.csreurope.org/uploadstore/cms/docs/CSRE_Pub_lifelonglearning_report.pdf + %E2%80%9CLifelong + Learning+at+the+Heart+of+an+Entrepreneurial+and+Inclusive+Europe%E2%80%9D&hl=en.

Eisen, Phyllis. National Association of Manufacturers. 2005. Presentation to Kansas City Association for Innovation Manufacturing, April 20.

Ford Foundation. 2005. Part of the solution: Leveraging business and markets for low-income people.

Forte Foundation. 2005. A good woman is hard to find: Women and networking. September 13. www.fortefoundation.org/site/PageServer?pagename = nw_center_3.

Horrigan, Michael. 2004. Employment projections to 2012: Concepts and context. U.S. Department of Labor, Bureau of Labor Statistics. *Monthly Labor Review* (February).

International Business Leaders Forum. 2005. Business in the community. June 13. www.princeofwales.gov.uk/trusts/business_comm.html.

Jobs for the Future. 2003. Hiring, retaining, and advancing front-line workers: A guide to successful human resources practices. www.jff.org/jff/library.

Jobs for the Future. 2004. WINs: Building capacity, producing results. November. www.jff.org/jff/PDFDocuments/WINsMarktFlyer.pdf.

Jobs for the Future. 2005. Education and skills for the 21st century: An agenda for action. www.jff.org/jff/library.

Jobs for the Future. 2006. Genesis Health Care case study.

National Association of Manufacturers. 2005. Dream it. Do it. cam paign. June 16. www.nam.org/s_nam/sec.asp?CID=201487&DID= 229867.

Sum, Andrew, Paul Harrington, and Ishwar Khatiwada. 2004. Analysis of immigrant contribution to labor market. Northeastern University Center for Labor Market Studies. January 9.

U.S. Chamber of Commerce. 2002. Theory of change for the Workforce Innovations Network. www.uschamber.com/NR/rdonlyres/e2ghl55i4 on7jjjbl2pgrruiu4djtdvvbwsfypikawhpjrjfo4244cuwxx6dlqmgda6v5hu efblu5e/winstheoryofchange.pdf.

U.S. Chamber of Commerce. 2003. Rising to the challenge: Business voices on the public workforce development system.

Weiser, John, and Simon Zadek. 2000. *Conversations with disbelievers: Persuading companies to address social challenges.* New York: Ford Foundation.

Whiting, Basil. 1997. Marriott's associate resource line. Case study prepared for Jobs for the Future. August.

Winning Workplaces. 2005. Correspondence on community partnerships. November 10.

Chapter 3: Increasing Value in the Supply Chain

Apco Worldwide, 2004. Communicating CSR: Talking to people who listen. Washington, DC: Author.

Arthur D. Little. 2003. The business case for corporate citizenship.

Asaba Group. 2005. Opportunities for minority suppliers in automotive industry.

The Body Shop. 2005. Financial releases. September 13. www.thebody shopinternational.com/web/tbsgl/news_financial.jsp.

Center for Corporate Citizenship at Boston College. 2001. Business and community development: Aligning corporate performance with community economic development to achieve win-win impacts.

Cone, Inc. 2002. Cone corporate citizenship report.

Deluca, Tom. 2003. How corporations are addressing poverty. Presentation to Center for Corporate Citizenship Conference. March.

Diversity Careers. 2005. Supplier diversity: DaimlerChrysler's 11 percent target includes Saturn Electronics. November 18. www.diversity careers.com/articles/pro/04-decjan/sd_daimler.htm.

The Economist. 2002. The road to hell is unpaved. *The Economist*, December 19.

Entine, Jon. 2002. Body flop. *Report on Business Magazine*, May 31.

Environics International. 1999. Executive briefing: The millennium poll on corporate social responsibility. September 30.

Environics International. 2002. 2002 corporate social responsibility monitor. May. www.globescan.com.

Fairtrade Labeling Organizations International. 2006. January 10. www.fair trade.net/sites/impact/facts.html.

Ford Motor Company. 2005. M-tier supplier diversity reporting system fact sheet. September 13. https://cvmas08.cvmsolutions.com/ford/CVM help/M-Tier_Fact_Sheet.pdf.

Gap, Inc. Gap code of conduct. November 18. http://gapinc.com/public/ SocialResponsibility/sr_ethic_cvc.shtml.

Hines, Lori, and Steven Larson. 2005. Conversation regarding Ford technical assistance program. August 23.

ICFA Center for Management Research. 2005. ICICI—Innovations in microfinance. Case was written by Indu P, under the direction of Vivek Gupta.

International Business Leaders Forum. 2002. The business of enterprise—Meeting the challenge of economic development through business and community partnerships. April.

Jacobs, Katy. 2004. Stored value cards: A scan of current trends and future opportunities. The Center for Financial Services Innovation. July.

Lester-Miller, Paula. 2004. Captains of innovation. *Minorities and Women in Business* (April/May) www.mwib.com/cover_april'04.htm.

National Minority Supplier Development Council. 2005a. Annual report 2003. August 1. www.nmsdcus.org/infocenter/NMSDC.Annual_Rpt .2003.pdf.

National Minority Supplier Development Council. 2005b. BCF impact statement. August 3. www.bcfcapital.com/impact.htm.

National Minority Supplier Development Council. 2005c. Who we are. August 2. www.nmsdcus.org/who_we_are/procurement.html.

Shell Petroleum Company of Nigeria. 2003. 2003 people and the environment: Annual report. www.shell.com/static/nigeria/downloads/pdfs/ annualreport_2003.pdf.

Texas Instruments. 2005. TI spending with MWBEs. September 13. www.ti .com/corp/docs/company/citizen/mwbd/history.shtml.

TransFair USA. 2005. TransFair USA: Making the US market work for farmers and farm workers worldwide. July.

Transparency International. 2005. Business principles for countering bribery. September 13. www.transparency.org/building_coalitions/private_sector/business_principles.html#steering.

Chapter 4: Accelerating Product and Process Innovation

Base of the Pyramid Protocol Project. 2005. Project description. August 25. www.bop-protocol.org.

Business in the Community. 2005. BBC–Oxford road project. November 18. www.bitc.org.uk/resources/case_studies/afe_660.html.

CEMEX. 2005. Building a better society. August 25. www.cemex.com/cc/cc_cc.asp.

Center for Corporate Citizenship at Boston College. 2004. In practice: Union Bank of California and Operation Hope. July.

Cornelius, Peter, Klaus Schwab, and Michael E. Porter. 2003. *The global competitiveness report, 2002–2003*. New York: Oxford University Press.

George, Michael L., James Works, and Kimberly Watson-Hemphill. 2005. *Fast Innovation*. New York: McGraw-Hill.

Hart, Stuart, and Clayton Christensen. 2002. The great leap. *MIT Sloan Management Review* (Fall).

Jacobs, Katy. 2004. Stored value cards: A scan of current trends and future opportunities. The Center for Financial Services Innovation. July.

Marshall, Craig. 2005. Personal correspondence.

One Economy. 2005. Hillary Clinton, One Economy and LISC/NEF announce $1 billion initiative. *One Economy Report* (August).

Reck, Jennifer, and Brad Wood. 2003. *What works: Vodacom's community services phone shops*. Washington, DC: World Resource Institute. August.

Rigby, Darrell, and Barbara Bilodeau. 2005. Management tools and trends 2005. Bain & Company.

Sabapathy, John, John Weiser, Claire Nacamuli, and Marjorie Polycarpe. 2003. Community-enabled innovation: Companies, communities, and innovation. *AccountAbility* (September).

Sandoval, Ricardo. 2005. Block by block: How one of the world's largest companies builds loyalty among Mexico's poor. *Stanford Social Innovation Review* (Summer).

Simanis, Eric, Stuart Hart, Gordon Enk, Duncan Duke, Michael Gordon, and Allyson Lippert. 2005. Strategic initiatives at the base of the pyramid: A protocol for mutual value creation. February 17.

U.S. Department of Housing and Urban Development. 2005. Low income housing tax credit database. August 30. www.huduser.org/datasets/lihtc.html.

Vision. 2005. Client stories. August 25. www.vision.com/clients/client_sto ries/cemex_pat.html5.

Weiser, John, and Simon Zadek. 2000. *Conversations with disbelievers: Persuading Companies to address social challenges.* New York: Ford Foundation.

World Business Council for Sustainable Development. 2005. Sustainable livelihoods. August 25. www.wbcsd.org/templates/TemplateWBCSD5/layout.asp?type = p&MenuId = Njc&doOpen = 1&ClickMenu = Left Menuttp.

Chapter 5: Building Partnerships That Work

Center for Corporate Citizenship at Boston College. 2002. In practice: Marriott case study. November.

Center for Corporate Citizenship at Boston College. 2003. In practice: Manpower case study. February.

Center for Corporate Citizenship at Boston College. 2004a. In practice: Green Mountain Coffee and TransFair. November.

Center for Corporate Citizenship at Boston College. 2004b. The state of corporate citizenship in the U.S. December.

Center for Corporate Citizenship at Boston College. 2004c. TJX Companies and Goodwill Industries join forces to make "Welfare to Work" work. March.

Ford Foundation. 2005. Part of the solution: Leveraging business and markets for low-income people.

Goodwill. 2005. Business collaborations: Success stories. September 15. www.goodwillmass.org/about_bc_success.html.

Laufer, Green, Isaac. 2004. Hidden agendas: Stereotypes and cultural barriers to corporate-community partnerships. February.

Lipponen, Kimmo. 2005. Correspondence Concerning Nokia Nonprofit Partnerships. October 13.

Manga, Julie Engel, and Sapna Shah. 2005. Enduring partnerships: Resilience, innovation, success. Center for Corporate Citizenship. February 16.

Rochlin, Steven, and Brad Googins. 2004. Defining the value proposition for corporate citizenship. Center for Corporate Citizenship at Boston College.

Simanis, Eric, Stuart Hart, Gordon Enk, Duncan Duke, Michael Gordon, and Allyson Lippert. 2005. Strategic initiatives at the base of the pyramid: A protocol for mutual value creation. February 17.

Chapter 6: Creating Value for Business and Community

Cohen, Joel E. 2005. Human population grows up. *Scientific American* (September).

❏ INDEX

■ ABOUT THE AUTHORS ■

John Weiser

John Weiser is a world-renowned expert on using business strategies to achieve both business and social goals, and has consulted widely with companies, foundations, and nonprofits on this subject. He has written numerous reports and books on the business case for corporate engagement with communities, including *Conversations With Disbelievers*, which examines the quantitative evidence for when and how corporate engagement with underserved communities creates bottom-line business benefits. He has led the process of creating, managing, and evaluating many corporate-nonprofit partnerships, including a number of those profiled in this book. He also was the lead consultant to the Ford Foundation Corporate Involvement Initiative, from which many cases in this book were drawn. John holds a master's degree in public and private management from the Yale School of Organization and Management.

John is a partner in the firm of Brody • Weiser • Burns, which he founded 20 years ago. The firm specializes in using business approaches to help achieve business and social goals.

Steve Rochlin

Steve Rochlin has spent more than ten years working with Fortune 500 businesses, and producing leading research on "win-win" models of corporate citizenship. As Director of Research and Policy Development for The Center for Corporate Citizenship at Boston College, Steve is responsible for supervising the Center's research initiatives. In this role, he has led research initiatives and coauthored many reports. Steve has also served as principal project manager on numerous consulting, strategic planning, and evaluation projects with the Center's members. In addition, he makes frequent presentations on corporate citizenship before leading national and international organizations.

The Center for Corporate Citizenship at Boston College is a membership-based research organization. It works with global corporations to help them define, plan, and operationalize their corporate citizenship. Its goal is to help business leverage its social, economic, and human assets to ensure both its success and a more just and sustainable world.

Prior to joining the Center, Steve worked extensively in the areas of technology-based economic development for both the National Academy of Sciences and the Center for Strategic and International Studies in Washington, D.C., and served as an associate for an economics and management consulting firm. He holds a master's in public policy from Harvard University's John F. Kennedy School of Government, and a bachelor of arts in political science from Brown University.

Michele Kahane

Michele Kahane joined the Center for Corporate Citizenship at Boston College in the fall of 2004. She consults with companies seeking to build more strategic corporate citizenship efforts. Michele is also playing a leading role at the Center to help companies leverage their core assets to develop breakthrough solutions to social challenges. Prior to working at the Center, Michele was a program officer in the Ford Foundation's Economic Development Unit for ten years. While there she managed the Corporate Involvement Initiative, which sought to leverage private sector resources on behalf of low-income communities. Her work has focused on building the global corporate social responsibility field and developing new business and governance models to address issues of poverty.

Prior to her work in philanthropy, she was a Vice President in Emerging Markets Corporate Finance at Chemical Bank. In addition, Michele worked for Catholic Relief Services. Michele holds a master of international affairs and master of business administration from Columbia University and a bachelor degree from Princeton University. She is currently on the advisory boards of the Women's Network for a Sustainable Future, the Institute for Responsible Investment, and the New York Regional Association of Grantmakers Task Force on Hurricane Katrina.

Jessica Landis

Jessica Landis is a Research Consultant at the Center for Corporate Citizenship at Boston College. She has contributed to a variety of projects including the Ford Foundation's *Learning Agenda*, the *Conversations With Disbelievers* Series, and the Center's In Practice

Database. She has also written several publications on a range of corporate citizenship topics, most notably a piece that examines the corporate citizenship integration processes and strategies at several global companies. Jessica holds a bachelor of arts from the University of Delaware and a master's from Boston College.

■ BE CONNECTED

Visit Our Website

Go to www.bkconnection.com to read exclusive previews and excerpts of new books, find detailed information on all Berrett-Koehler titles and authors, browse subject-area libraries of books, and get special discounts.

Subscribe to Our Free E-Newsletter

Be the first to hear about new publications, special discount offers, exclusive articles, news about bestsellers, and more! Get on the list for our free e-newsletter by going to www.bkconnection.com.

Participate in the Discussion

To see what others are saying about our books and post your own thoughts, check out our blogs at www.bkblogs.com.

Get Quantity Discounts

Berrett-Koehler books are available at quantity discounts for orders of ten or more copies. Please call us toll-free at (800) 929-2929 or email us at bkp.orders@aidcvt.com.

Host a Reading Group

For tips on how to form and carry on a book reading group in your workplace or community, see our website at www.bkconnection .com.

Join the BK Community

Thousands of readers of our books have become part of the "BK Community" by participating in events featuring our authors, reviewing draft manuscripts of forthcoming books, spreading the word about their favorite books, and supporting our publishing program in other ways. If you would like to join the BK Community, please contact us at bkcommunity@bkpub.com.